THE NORTON SERIES ON
SOCIAL EMOTIONAL LEARNING SOLUTIONS
PATRICIA A. JENNINGS, SERIES EDITOR

*Mindfulness in the Secondary Classroom: A Guide for
Teaching Adolescents*
Patricia C. Broderick

*SEL Every Day: Integrating Social and Emotional Learning
with Instruction in Secondary Classrooms*
Meena Srinivasan

*Assessing Students' Social and Emotional Learning:
A Guide to Meaningful Measurement*
Clark McKown

*Mindfulness in the PreK–5 Classroom:
Helping Students Stress Less and Learn More*
Patricia A. Jennings

*Preventing Bullying in Schools:
A Social and Emotional Learning Approach to Early Intervention*
Catherine P. Bradshaw and Tracy Evian Waasdorp

NORTON BOOKS IN EDUCATION

Advance Praise

"This is the best book I have read on practical approaches to assess students' social and emotional learning (SEL). It informs district and school administrators, teachers, and student-support personnel on how to measure students' social and emotional strengths and to use data to enhance students' behavior and school success. This is a valuable pre-service and in-service training resource for practitioners who implement school-family strategies to measure and promote SEL."

—**Roger P. Weissberg, Ph.D., Chief Knowledge Officer, Collaborative for Academic, Social, and Emotional Learning (CASEL), UIC Distinguished Professor Emeritus of Psychology, University of Illinois at Chicago**

"If we take the importance of SEL skills seriously, we must find ways to assess these skills and provide teachers and leaders with accurate and actionable data. This book offers practical advice that can help leaders choose the right SEL assessment tools and, most importantly, use them in ways that can transform students' daily experiences in the classroom. A must-read for any leader working on SEL reforms!"

—**Bridget Hamre, Ph.D., Research Associate Professor, University of Virginia, author of *The Classroom Assessment Scoring System (CLASS)***

"Clark McKown provides an outstanding overview of why assessing SEL is so important. In doing so he has created a much-needed practical guide for educators and parents on why we should assess SEL, what we might assess, how we can assess, and how we can use the information that is generated. Bravo!"

—**Paul Goren, Ph.D., Superintendent of Schools, Evanston/Skokie (IL) District 65 and Board Member of CASEL and the New Teachers Center**

"Dr. McKown has done it! This book provides clear and specific guidance to assess social and emotional learning skills for our students. A meaningful and astute must-read for any school principal or district level leader struggling with the next steps to support intentional work in SEL. I wish we'd had this resource as we started our journey several years ago!"

—**Catherine Wang, Ed.D., Superintendent of Schools, Glencoe District 35**

Assessing Students' Social and Emotional Learning

A Guide to Meaningful Measurement

Clark McKown

W. W. Norton & Company

Independent Publishers Since 1923

New York London

Note to Readers: Models and/or techniques described in this volume are illustrative or are included for general informational purposes only; neither the publisher nor the author(s) can guarantee the efficacy or appropriateness of any particular recommendation in every circumstance.

For information about permission to reproduce selections from this book, write to Permissions, W. W. Norton & Company, Inc., 500 Fifth Avenue, New York, NY 10110

For information about special discounts for bulk purchases, please contact W. W. Norton Special Sales at specialsales@wwnorton.com or 800-233-4830

Manufacturing by Versa Press
Book design by Molly Heron
Production manager: Katelyn MacKenzie

Library of Congress Cataloging-in-Publication Data

Names: McKown, Clark, author.
Title: Assessing students' social and emotional learning :
a guide to meaningful measurement / Clark McKown.
Description: First edition. | New York : W.W. Norton & Company, [2019] |
Series: Norton books in education | Series: Social emotional learning solutions series |
Includes bibliographical references and index.
Identifiers: LCCN 2018050516 | ISBN 9780393713350 (pbk.)
Subjects: LCSH: Affective education. | Social learning. | Emotional intelligence. |
Psychological tests for children.
Classification: LCC LB1072 .M385 2019 | DDC 370.15/34—dc23
LC record available at https://lccn.loc.gov/2018050516

W. W. Norton & Company, Inc., 500 Fifth Avenue, New York, N.Y. 10110
www.wwnorton.com

W. W. Norton & Company Ltd., 15 Carlisle Street, London W1D 3BS

1 2 3 4 5 6 7 8 9 0

For Beth and Kate

Contents

From the Series Editor ix
Introduction xv

1   What Is Social and Emotional Learning? 1

2   Why Assess Children's SEL? 16

3   Selecting the Right Tool for the Job 27

4   Engaging Parents as Partners 55

5   Using the Data 66

6   **The Future of SEL Assessment**   92

References   97
Index   101

From the Series Editor

The SOCIAL AND EMOTIONAL LEARNING SOLUTIONS (SEL SOLU-
TIONS) SERIES features compact books for educators focused on rec-
ommended SEL practices from experts in the field. Cutting-edge research
continues to confirm that teaching students social and emotional skills pays
off in improved behavior and academic learning that continues into adult-
hood as success in life. The books are intended to provide school leaders
and classroom teachers with SEL tools and strategies that are grounded in
research yet highly accessible, so readers can confidently begin using them
to transform school culture, improve student behavior, and foster learning
with the proven benefits of SEL.

I am delighted to introduce Clark McKown's new book *Assessing Students' Social and Emotional Learning.* As a former teacher and school leader,
I questioned my informal assessments of my students' social and emotional
skills. For example, I might think "It seems like he's really having trou-

ble making friends, but I think maybe one of the other kids is bullying him when I'm not looking. I'm going to have to watch them more closely." Or, "She seems emotionally immature for her age, but maybe she's having other problems at home. I need to speak to her parents, but I'm not sure what to say."

As I transitioned into teacher education, the importance of social and emotional development was just beginning to be recognized in the field of education. My early bias emphasized academic learning over social and emotional learning. However, when I became a parent, I saw firsthand how our son's academic success actually depended upon his social and emotional skills. I shifted the focus of my work on social and emotional development and found a growing field of practice and research that was just beginning to be articulated. During these early phases, I found the contrasting and overlapping theoretical models and frameworks were confusing. As a practitioner, it was difficult to review the research to learn how best to apply it to improving practice. It was even more difficult to figure out how to assess SEL.

When I became a researcher, I began to explore assessment issues from a research perspective. As a former teacher, it became all too clear that education researchers often miss the mark on understanding how assessment can be most helpful for those who need it for improving practice, not just conducting basic research. When I discovered Clark McKown's work, I was thrilled that he had worked so closely with educators to make his work relevant to improving practice and at the same time conducting rigorous research. As soon as this series was initiated, I invited him to contribute a book on assessment.

Assessing Students' Social and Emotional Learning exceeds my already-high expectations. Written in a friendly, accessible style with anecdotes from personal experience, the book synthesizes what we know about best practices in high-impact SEL assessment and offers step-by-step guidance for school leadership and educators. McKown applies a strength-based approach that considers SEL skills within the framework of a multi-tiered system of support (MTSS).

The book will not only help educators understand what SEL skills are and which skills matter most in the school context, but will also provide a roadmap for deciding on assessment goals and choosing tools to help achieve them. Importantly, the book provides guidance on how to define skills in such a way that they can be easily assessed, and on how to interpret and use assessment data for continuous improvement. As both a parent and an educator, I appreciate the chapter on building supportive partnerships with parents, to engage them in the process. *Assessing Students' Social and Emotional Learning* fills an important need that is too often overlooked: evidence-based yet accessible guidance for educators developing SEL programming and assessment systems. As the author points out, assessing students' SEL skills can be a potent means to focus instruction and improve student outcomes, as long as the assessment is designed with clear goals in mind and the resulting data is interpreted carefully and used as the basis for an action plan.

Patricia A. Jennings, M.Ed., Ph.D.
Editor, Norton Series on Social and Emotional Learning Solutions

Introduction

This book is mainly for district and school administrators and other educators who want to engage in high-impact student SEL assessment, which refers to assessing student social and emotional learning (SEL) skill in a way that meaningfully informs practice and improves student outcomes. Achieving high-impact student SEL assessment requires much more than an assessment tool. In fact, a key premise of this book is that the assessment tool is just one element of a larger process. For a student SEL assessment tool to make a difference—in how educators understand their students, in how teachers support student learning, and in student outcomes—requires a series of events and, often, changes to systems and ways of thinking.

High-impact student SEL assessment includes careful planning that includes defining what student SEL skills are most important, clarifying the goals of undertaking assessment, selecting the right assessment tool to assess what matters most and to achieve the assessment goals. It also involves enlisting parents as partners and, after student SEL assessment data are collected, creating opportunities for educators to reflect on, discuss, and take positive action based on assessment findings. Assessment, in this sense, is a complex process that includes the assessment tool and many other important elements. This book aspires to support educators who want to maximize the impact of their SEL assessment initiative, from planning through action.

Student SEL Assessment: Simple but Not Easy and Always Fascinating

This book originates from a simple but not easy question that has consistently animated my work—How do children understand their world, particularly the social world? What do they make of the strange and complex behavior of their fellow humans, big and small? What do they know, and when and how do they know, what is in the minds and hearts of others? How do their ideas about and understanding of others influence their ideas about themselves? How do they figure out how to make their way through complex social situations? How in the world do they coordinate the intricate mosaic of their own behavior with that of others? And how can we adults assess children's understanding of the social world in ways that give us insights we can use to support their growth and development?

My curiosity about how the youngest among us think about, understand, and interact with others has led me down a fascinating and engaging career path. Specifically, my work has largely focused on figuring out how to ask children questions that give us the best shot at understanding how they understand their social worlds and supporting their development. At first blush, this seems like a trivial problem, to which one might blithely say, "Just ask!" But children, particularly young children, understand the world in ways that are profoundly different than the ways we do. What might seem a trivial problem with adults becomes, with children, complicated and endlessly interesting.

For example, to understand the social skills of a reasonably self-aware and candid adult, it might suffice to ask about his or her relationships and social skills. But among children, that simply won't do precisely because they understand themselves and the world differently than do adults. And so my career has evolved into developing the kinds of developmentally appropriate tasks and questions that, when all goes well, give us a window into children's understanding of the social world. For the past decade and a half or so, this has been reflected in a concerted effort to develop and adapt methods of assessing children's social and emotional learning skills, by which I mean the thinking skills, behaviors, and regulatory processes needed to interact effectively with others and to make and maintain positive relationships.

For many years, I focused mainly on the task of developing technically sound SEL assessments. But then something funny happened on the way to the schoolhouse. My colleagues and I were getting ready to mount a large school-based field trial of our first social and emotional assessment system, which was designed to measure important skills in children from kindergarten to third grade, including how well they understand others' emotions and perspectives, solve social problems, and engage in self-control. As is often our habit in the university, we developed this assessment system because we thought these were important skills and we wanted to demonstrate that they could be meaningfully and feasibly administered to large numbers of students.

The spring before the field trial, I began meeting with educators—mostly principals and district-level decision makers. The plan was to ask for permission to work with maybe 10% of students to collect data that would help us understand how well the assessment worked. I described what we were doing and braced myself for what I thought would be a tepid response from educators wary of researchers. But to my utter surprise, most of the educators I approached did not say no. Far from it—most expressed a strong interest in understanding their children's social and emotional skills better. They wanted to administer the assessment to all children and for us to share with them what we learned to help them understand their students and make decisions about programming and instruction based on what they learned.

I am not the kind of person who regularly has lightbulb moments. However, these conversations were a revelation. In devising ways to assess social and emotional skills, my colleagues and I had stumbled upon what appeared to be a great unmet need, and the excitement of our education partners was infectious. Before, the thrill of the work was in creating an assessment with sound technical properties. Now, that thrill was in creating an assessment that could answer questions that many people want answered, that could create insights, and that could spur positive action. Yes, the technical soundness of assessments remained important, but only if the technically sound assessment fulfilled a larger purpose—the purpose of contributing to a greater good. In short, my focus shifted from building tools that work to building tools that matter.

It was around that time that I decided that I would no longer do research for its own sake, but would dedicate my energies to doing research, in collaboration with educators, that advances practice while maintaining scientific rigor. In the wake of that change in focus, I have learned some very important lessons. As I have not worked out the answers entirely, perhaps it is more accurate to say some very important challenges have become clear to me—challenges with which I continue to grapple and that are in large part the focus of this book. The crux is this: On the one hand, educators have expressed a consistent and strong desire, dare I say a hunger, to be able to assess the social and emotional skills they are working so assiduously to teach. On the other hand, educators' enthusiasm for assessing SEL often outpaces their clarity about what they want to measure, why they want to measure it, what assessments are available to achieve their goals, how to partner with parents in the SEL assessment project, and what to do once the assessment data are collected.

The Challenges

The challenges are interrelated but partially distinct. They are difficult, but addressable. Let's take them one at a time.

1. The first challenge is that many educators want to assess (and address)

children's social and emotional strengths and needs, but they are unsure what SEL is. Is it grit? Relationship skills? Responsible decision-making? Character? Or is it something else altogether? Educators have good reason to be confused as the field continues to wrestle with basic questions about what SEL is and what it is not. I discuss the vexing issue of defining SEL in Chapter 1. Spoiler alert 1: I haven't worked out the Tower of Babel problem facing the field, but I do try to offer some practical ways to sort through it all in ways that I hope will help educators clarify what SEL skills matter most to them. Spoiler alert 2: This book approaches social-emotional learning from a strengths perspective in which student SEL skills are positive outcomes we want to nurture; this volume does not focus on pathology or student deficiencies.

2. The second challenge concerns clarity of purpose for undertaking assessment. Assessment can be undertaken for many reasons, explored in detail in Chapter 2, including formative assessment, summative assessment, screening and identification, diagnosis, program evaluation, accountability, and progress monitoring, to name a few. Clarity of purpose is an important precondition for high-impact assessment, because (1) it increases the odds that the assessment endeavor will achieve a specific and valued goal, (2) it facilitates clear communication to audiences involved in and affected by SEL assessment, and (3) it reduces the chances that assessment data will be used in unanticipated and potentially harmful ways.

Achieving goal clarity is more difficult than it might seem. Unlike achievement testing, whose purpose is largely prescribed by policy, SEL assessment is not typically undertaken in response to a policy requirement. Because it is not required nor are its goals prescribed, the onus for defining the assessment goals falls on educators. At the same time, within a school district, different educators may have different goals in mind when undertaking social and emotional assessment. For example, district leaders may want to monitor student SEL skill development over time as they roll out an SEL program. General education teachers might wish to use SEL assessment data to help them make decisions about what and how to teach to build on student strengths and address student needs. Special educators may wish to use SEL assessment data to identify children with noteworthy deficits to guide Tier 2 or 3 intervention planning. Goal clarity, or lack thereof, can have dramatic consequences for how—and how well—assessment data are used to inform instruction and support student learning.

3. The third challenge educators face, even those who are crystal clear about what they want to assess and why they want to assess it, is identifying high-quality assessments designed to assess high-priority social and emotional skills and that are capable of helping achieve specific assessment goals. Imagine, for example, you were a principal who felt that it was important to assess social awareness, one of five core SEL skills described by the Collaborative for Academic Social and Emotional Learning, or CASEL. Imagine further that you understood social awareness to consist of understanding others' thoughts and feelings and respecting diversity of opinion and background. Imagine you were committed to assessing your students' social awareness and to using what you learned to decide on professional development and program investments. So far, so good. Except for one thing. It is far from clear what assessments are available to measure social awareness. It is not even clear where to turn to identify appropriate assess-

ment resources, although that is changing. And it is not easy to evaluate the technical qualities of assessments. Chapter 3 takes up the challenge of selecting the right assessment tool for the job.

4. The fourth challenge is enlisting parents as partners in undertaking student SEL assessment. Many parents become nervous about the idea that their children's social-emotional skills will be assessed. At the same time, parents have an enormous influence on children's social and emotional development and the more coordinated parents and teachers are in their efforts to support student social and emotional development, the better. Chapter 4 explores some of the most common parent concerns and offers ideas about how educators can address those concerns and join with parents to ensure that home and school are working in harmony to support student SEL.

5. The fifth challenge is what to do with the assessment data once they are collected. It is possible, with focused effort, to be clear about what one wants to assess and why and about what tools will be used to accomplish those assessment goals. Unless the assessment data are used, however, they won't do anyone any good. When the assessment data are collected, and scores are in hand, there is the problem one education colleague described succinctly as, "So what? Now what?" "So what?" refers to the problem of what the assessment data mean. Score reports can be daunting, and all educators want to be able to understand the meaning behind the numbers. What skill does each reflect? What do the numbers tell us about student social and emotional skill level? What questions do the assessment data raise about students?

If "So what?" is about interpreting assessment data, "Now what?" is about what to do with the insights. Most people go into education because they want their actions to make a positive difference in children's lives. It is not enough just to know how well-developed children's social and emotional skills are. Educators also want to know how to use what they learn to chart a course of action that will build on student strengths and address student needs. For assessment data to inform teaching and learning, and for educators to answer the questions "So what?" and "Now what?" several things must be in place. Chapter 5 describes the conditions of effective SEL assessment data use and how to create them.

What to Expect From This Book

These challenges are difficult, but they can be met. The goal of this book is to offer practical guidance to address these five challenges so that educators can mount high-impact SEL assessment initiatives. The book assumes that assessment will be universal—that is, all children's social and emotional learning skills will be assessed. This emphasis arises from my belief that SEL assessment should generally not be limited to screening and identification of children at risk, or exclusively for assessing the strengths and challenges of children with special needs. When educators wisely assess all children's social and emotional learning skills, what they learn about students' strengths and needs can help them be more effective educators, leading to a measurable benefit for all students.

This book focuses mainly on assessment in the elementary school years. That focus reflects the greater emphasis in the education system on SEL in the early grades and my own expertise. As a result, this book may be of greatest interest to elementary educators. However, SEL skills are important throughout a child's educational career and beyond. Anyone who doubts this should recall the challenges and complexities of high school social life, and it will become clear that social and emotional skills play a central role in navigating the often-choppy waters of adolescence. In that spirit, my hope is that the ideas in this volume are relevant and helpful to educators at all grade levels.

This book takes a strengths-based approach to SEL. That is, a guiding premise of this book is that student SEL skills are positive outcomes that we can (and should) assess and address. This book does not treat SEL as the absence of pathologies such as anxiety, depression, conduct problems, or other disorders of childhood. I recognize that child psychopathology is a very important subject, and in fact, my training is in clinical psychology. But this book does not deal with psychopathology or deficit. Instead, it focuses on the social and emotional skills students need to navigate social interactions and collective life, in the classroom and in the community. The most direct connection between SEL and deficit is this: The more equipped children are with SEL skills, the less likely they are to develop a mental illness.

This book focuses on *student* SEL skill assessment, not social-emotional climate or adult practices. I focus on student skills for a couple of reasons. First, I believe that the best instruction is informed by knowledge of what students know and can do, and what they don't yet know and cannot do. Most would take it on faith that knowledge of individual student reading and math skills, obtained through high quality assessment, is a key tool in the educator's toolkit without which it would be difficult to be effective. In my view, the same is true when it comes to SEL skills. I believe that teachers committed to supporting student social and emotional development can use student SEL skill assessment to be more effective. Second, some argue that it is more important to assess the social-emotional climate or teacher practices that influence social and emotional development, and fear that a focus on student skills may lead us to neglect improving adult practices. Too often, this argument is posed in a zero-sum way that implies you must choose between assessing student SEL skills and assessing adult practices. In the best of all worlds, educators will assess student SEL skills *and* the conditions of learning, because in fact, they are intimately related. Third, many argue that the field is not yet ready to assess student SEL skills in beneficial ways because of the risk of unintended harm. I agree there are important considerations to maximize benefit and minimize risk. However, like many educators, I believe student SEL assessment can and should be a useful and beneficial educational tool. This book offers strategies to use student SEL assessment thoughtfully. Along the way, it describes potential hazards and discusses ways to mitigate risk.

To many educators, the world of student SEL assessment may seem arcane, impractical, and perhaps intimidating. However, exciting developments are making SEL assessment more accessible and useful than ever. The main goal of this book is to provide educators with practical information they can use to mount a high-impact SEL assessment initiative. This book is designed to help educators think through the key challenges of identifying and prioritizing the most important SEL skills, clarifying assessment goals, selecting the right assessment tools for the job, enlisting parents as partners, and using SEL assessment data to benefit teaching and learning. Written primarily for elementary administrators and teachers, it will provide educators with practical information they can use to

1. decide what dimensions of SEL are most important to them,
2. clarify their assessment goals,
3. identify viable assessment options that meet their needs,
4. join with parents as partners, and
5. understand and use assessment data to inform their practice.

Part of the solution to the challenges facing educators interested in SEL assessment involves the technical features of assessments such as score reliability and validity for a particular purpose. These are important considerations. However, wise assessment involves more than grasping the technical properties of assessments—it requires leadership, socializing the importance of and reasons for assessment, systems-change efforts, and building-level routines and practices for reviewing assessment data to grasp the facts they reflect, deliberate over their meaning, and make decisions about what to do based on the data. A differentiating feature of this book is the equal emphasis given to planning for SEL assessment, selecting the assessment itself, and the process of reviewing, making sense of, and using assessment data to make decisions about practice. The ambition of this book is to help educators bridge the gap between SEL assessment data and educational practice in ways that help them do their jobs effectively, and that in turn benefit students.

The Chapters to Come

Chapter 1 offers guidance to educators on the process of deciding what elements of SEL are most important in the local context. The chapter starts by discussing some common definitions of SEL. Broadly, this book is focused on the skills that children need to interact successfully with others, and to develop and maintain positive relationships. This definition is child focused and does not include other important related ideas like the classroom climate. The definition is also skills focused, emphasizing those thinking and behavioral skills that are meaningful, measurable, and malleable. However, these are very broad terms, and educators who want to mount a high-impact SEL assessment program will need to spend time and effort focusing on the elements of SEL that are most important to them. Chapter 1 provides practical guidance on how to get to clarity about what elements of SEL are most important.

Chapter 2 focuses on the goals of assessment. Assessments themselves are dumb—they provide data about skills, but they don't care how we use them. As a result, assessment data can be used to achieve many goals such as formative assessment, continuous improvement, program evaluation, and more. To ensure that all involved in and affected by SEL assessment are engaged in common purpose and communicate clearly—and to ensure that

SEL assessment has maximum benefit and minimal risk—it is important to be clear about what the goal of SEL assessment is (and is not). This chapter explores the varied goals to which SEL assessment can be applied, and the steps educators can take to come to the level of goal clarity necessary for high-impact SEL assessment.

Chapters 1 and 2 describe how to clarify what SEL skills are most important and the goals for assessing them, which lays important groundwork for selecting the right assessment tool for the job. That is the focus of Chapter 3. This chapter reviews the different methods of assessment and their strengths and limitations for assessing different kinds of SEL skill. It also provides a consumer's guide to evaluating the technical properties of assessments, guidance about how to evaluate the fit between what you want to measure and why, and the technical properties of the assessment tools you are considering.

Although most people agree that SEL skills are important, parents are sometimes uneasy when educators focus on SEL, and particularly when they *assess* SEL skills. They may have a number of important concerns ranging from the possibility of stigma, to concerns that assessments may cover sensitive and intrusive material, to worry about the cultural appropriateness of SEL assessment. Chapter 4 examines common parent concerns and discusses actions educators can take to enlist parents as partners in the assessment of SEL skills.

When all the data are gathered, the job is done, right? Wrong. Chapter 5 discusses what must happen after the assessment to ensure that assessment data are reviewed, interpreted, discussed, and used as the basis for decisions about teaching and learning. The chapter offers a definition of data use that goes beyond the kinds of cursory reviews of assessment data that can severely limit the impact of those data. The chapter also discusses how the key elements of data use can be put into practice.

Finally, Chapter 6 discusses emerging developments in the field of SEL assessment and anticipates future changes.

Assessing Students' Social and Emotional Learning

What Is Social and Emotional Learning?

Social and emotional learning means different things to different people. Regardless of who you ask, though, most agree that SEL includes a complex set of interrelated skills. Assessing every element of SEL is, in most cases, impractical and even undesirable. And so the first challenge for educators who want to undertake high-impact SEL assessment is deciding what SEL skills are most important to them. This involves convening a team in the district to review existing models of SEL to identify the specific SEL skills that, if improved, would make the biggest difference in the lives of students. This process involves: (1) deciding who should be involved in identifying what SEL skills matter most, (2) selecting an SEL model as a starting point, (3) deciding what specific skills from that model matter most in your community, (4) classifying each skill in a way that lends itself to assessment, and (5) finalizing the list of SEL skills you will prioritize for assessment and instruction.

A Daunting but Doable Task

Before we dive into defining SEL, I have a confession: I avoided sitting down to write this chapter for longer than I care to admit. When I finally enlisted some emotion regulation strategies (a few deep breaths and some positive self-talk) and perched myself in my favorite coffee shop to start writing, I became aware of a distinct feeling: anxiety. And as I reflected upon the source of the anxiety, it didn't take much to figure out that the topic of this chapter was its source. Maybe you are surprised that what seems like it should be a simple task—defining some terms to lay the groundwork for what's to come—is instead the source of the jitters and no small amount of avoidance. There's a reason for this, which I describe below.

But first, as I ready myself to delve into this great tangle of ideas, let me say that I suspect at least some of you will be tempted to skip this part. Of course, I encourage you to stick it out. On the off chance that you decide to skip ahead, let me start with the most important message of this chapter: As you consider what you want to do to nurture children's SEL—and particularly as you consider how you want to assess it—please spend the time and effort needed to be clear about what you and your colleagues mean by SEL. This will affect how you choose to assess and address SEL in your district. Coming to clarity about what SEL means sounds easy; it's not. Here's the test I propose: If everyone in your school or district, asked independently to define SEL, supplied the same definition—what it is, what it looks like, how it is measured, and what the main strategies are for achieving it—you've arrived. Bonus points for listing commonly discussed dimensions of SEL that are *not* the focus of your school or district, because this demonstrates a keen awareness not just of what you've come to agree SEL is, but also what it isn't.

It will likely take more time and effort than you anticipate getting to this level of clarity. What's the big deal, you say? Well, achieving this standard of clarity is difficult because there are, in fact dozens of models, frameworks, theories, and definitions laying claim to the term "social and emotional learning." It may seem that the proliferation of models is an esoteric matter unrelated to practice. It is not. A clear definition of SEL stakes a claim about what is and what is not important. Getting to clarity facilitates communication by ensuring that everyone involved has a common understanding of what SEL is, what it isn't, why it matters, and how they can influence it. An SEL assessment initiative without a clear definition is like a ship without a rudder—it might find its way to port, but is more likely to founder.

The Team for the Job

First, bring together the team who will be responsible for developing a clear and functional operational definition of SEL for your district. Each district will decide who should lead and who should be involved in this work and the composition of the group will depend on local considerations. If you share my bias that SEL and its assessment is important for all students, then it will be important that general educators play a key role in this process. The most successful initiative will have the support of the district cabinet member in charge of curriculum and instruction. With his or her support, a small committee will be charged with studying models of SEL and working together, with input from colleagues, to identify the most important SEL skills described in that model. They will take their work back to district leadership for approval. This will set the stage for all the assessment and programming to come. And in fact, this is also probably the right team to clarify assessment goals (Chapter 2), and to select the right tool for the job (Chapter 3).

The SEL Tower of Babel Problem

One challenge when undertaking this task is the proliferation of theories, models, and definitions of SEL. Each encompasses its own idea of what skills are part of SEL and, by implication, what skills are not part of SEL. Each model generally originates from an identifiable subgroup of academics who developed the model as part of a lifelong program of work. Most models are well justified by bodies of evidence that the skills they describe can be taught and are associated with outcomes we care about. Often different terms have similar meanings (see "grit" and "self-management"). Other times, the same term—SEL—appears to refer to largely distinct things (see "growth mind-set" and "relationship management"). Each theory, in short, makes a distinct set of claims about what SEL is, why it matters, and what can be done to influence its development, using its own terminology. To avoid confusion and anchor the discussion about what matters most, the first task of the group charged with coming to a clear operational definition of SEL is to identify one model or theory as a starting point.

To that end, it may be useful to consider some of the more influential "big-tent" models as a starting point. By that I mean commonly cited models that incorporate a broad range of skills within an organizing system. The Collaborative for Academic Social and Emotional Learning, also known as CASEL, describes five major components of SEL: self-awareness, social awareness, self-management, relationship skills, and responsible decision-making. A variety of skills fit under each of these five broad areas. Figure 1.1 describes each of the five areas and some of the skills that fall under each.

There are other models of SEL in addition to CASEL's. One describes noncognitive factors such as academic mind-sets, learning strategies, and social skills (Nagaoka, Farrington, Ehrlich, & Heath, 2015). Another describes 21st-century skills, including intrapersonal, interpersonal, and cognitive skills (National Research Council, 2012). Jones and Bouffard (2012) described a model of SEL that includes emotional and social/interpersonal skills, and contextual factors that influence the development of those skills. Others emphasize information processing (Lemirese & Arsinio, 2000), neu-

Self-awareness

The ability to accurately recognize one's own emotions, thoughts, and values and how they influence behavior. The ability to accurately assess one's strengths and limitations, with a well-grounded sense of confidence, optimism, and a "growth mindset."

- Identifying emotions
- Accurate self-perception
- Recognizing strengths
- Self-confidence
- Self-efficacy

Self-management

The ability to successfully regulate one's emotions, thoughts, and behaviors in different situations — effectively managing stress, controlling impulses, and motivating oneself. The ability to set and work toward personal and academic goals.

- Impulse control
- Stress management
- Self-discipline
- Self-motivation
- Goal-setting
- Organizational skills

Social awareness

The ability to take the perspective of and empathize with others, including those from diverse backgrounds and cultures. The ability to understand social and ethical norms for behavior and to recognize family, school, and community resources and supports.

- Perspective-taking
- Empathy
- Appreciating diversity
- Respect for others

Relationship skills

The ability to establish and maintain healthy and rewarding relationships with diverse individuals and groups. The ability to communicate clearly, listen well, cooperate with others, resist inappropriate social pressure, negotiate conflict constructively, and seek and offer help when needed.

- Communication
- Social engagement
- Relationship-building
- Teamwork

Responsible decision-making

The ability to make constructive choices about personal behavior and social interactions based on ethical standards, safety concerns, and social norms. The realistic evaluation of consequences of various actions, and a consideration of the well-being of oneself and others.

- Identifying problems
- Analyzing situations
- Solving problems
- Evaluating
- Reflecting
- Ethical responsibility

FIGURE 1.1: Core SEL Competencies (https://casel.org/core-competencies/)

Source: Collaborative for Academic, Social, and Emotional Learning (©CASEL) www.casel.org

ropsychological processes (Beauchamp & Anderson, 2010), or emotional processes (Halberstadt, Denham, & Dunsmore, 2001). The list goes on.

The CASEL model is a big tent in that it includes a great many skills, organized under broad categories that are intuitively accessible to an educated lay audience. Its usefulness is evident in its wide adoption. Most visibly, for example, a growing number of states are adopting standards for the SEL skills that children should know and be able to demonstrate at each grade level (Dusenbury, Dermody, & Weissberg, 2018). A cursory inspection of state SEL standards makes it clear that policy makers are using CASEL's model to craft specific benchmarks. In addition, the skills in the CASEL model are commonly the target of instruction in widely-used SEL programs.

Your first task, then, is to select the model of SEL you find most compelling to use as the starting point in your work to define which SEL skills matter most. You will use this model as both an anchor and a menu. It will anchor you to a broad, but also finite and manageable, set of SEL skills to consider. In this way, the model you select will represent your first step towards clarity by making a commitment to the skills that the chosen model describes, but not skills described in other models. Refer to the model to bring things back into focus if your discussion of the SEL skills that matter most starts to get fuzzy. It will also be a menu of skill domains and specific skills. From this menu, you can select SEL skills that are most important to your district. Often, selecting from the menu will be a starting point, and will require further clarification. You may decide, for example, that "social awareness" from the CASEL model is important. You'll have to reframe this in usable terms so that you can plan to assess and address that important skill. How you do that is the subject of the rest of the chapter.

A Useful Way to Organize the SEL Skills That Matter Most

Let's imagine that you decide to start with the CASEL model. Your challenge now is to extract from this expansive model a working definition of social and emotional learning that clarifies what skills matter most to your community. And so, at the risk of adding yet another way of thinking about SEL to the already crowded field of contenders, I offer a definition of SEL designed not to compete with the CASEL model, or any other, but to help educators come to clarity about what it is, after all, that they care about most and want to assess and address. This definition of SEL skills is particularly useful in thinking about assessment because it tends to arrange SEL skills from models like CASEL's into categories that point towards assessment strategies. Specifically, it is useful to think of SEL as *the thinking skills, behavioral skills, and self-control skills children need to interact successfully with peers and adults and to make, maintain, and deepen relationships.* In your review of a broad SEL model, this definition can organize high-priority SEL skills in a way that will help you plan assessment and other programming. The key is the three kinds of skills described in this definition: comprehension (or thinking skills), execution (or behavioral skills), and self-control. Let's take them one at a time.

Comprehension

Comprehension includes thinking skills—the largely invisible stuff that happens between the ears, including children's ability to read social cues, understand themselves and others, and think through social challenges. These skills have no outward sign. Take an example of a child who is looking at other children on the playground and making all kinds of inferences about how the other children feel from their body language and about what they intend by the context. The child's mind is engaging in very active thinking about these matters, but from the outside, one would be hard pressed to know whether and how well the child was reading cues about others' emotions and intentions. This extensive mental activity is happening with little corresponding outward behavior to betray any specifics. These skills have been usefully called "social and emotional comprehension" (Lipton & Nowicki, 2009). It includes things like the ability to read nonverbal cues about others' emotions, to take others' perspectives, and to solve social problems.

Execution

The second kind of skill involves observable actions in the context of interpersonal interactions. This includes things like smiling and nodding in a conversation, using descriptive and emphatic gestures when telling a story, taking turns on the playground, and stating an opinion assertively and respectfully. These kinds of socially positive behaviors facilitate positive interactions and tend to lead to positive relationships and other desirable outcomes (DiPerna, Volpe, & Elliott, 2002; Newcomb, Bukowski, & Patee, 1993). Social behavior can also include aversive acts that contribute to negative interactions and undermine relationships, including things like yelling, hitting, saying hurtful things, spreading rumors, avoiding others, failing to make eye contact, and interrupting. Socially aversive behaviors are not, of course, skills. However, refraining from those behaviors does imply a level of skill. Collectively, the actions (positive and negative) that people take to achieve social goals are social and emotional execution.

Self-Control

A third kind of social and emotional skill involves self-control, including the mental and behavioral strategies children use to regulate their thoughts, feelings, and behaviors during social interactions. This is a rather complex area, and the specific skills that are most important and how they work together is not yet completely worked out. However, most would agree, and research finds, that self-control is an important skill for success in school, life, relationships, careers, and all manner of endeavors (Moffitt et al., 2011). Self-control is distinct from comprehension and execution but includes mental and behavioral components. The mental aspects of self-control include cognitive strategies for staying calm when upsetting things happen—like reframing a problem as an opportunity or using self-talk to keep perspective (Gross, 1998). Its opposite is emotional dysregulation, which is often experienced as feeling upset, often out of proportion to events. The behavioral aspects of self-control include knowing when to refrain from behaviors that might be aversive and knowing when to engage in socially positive behavior. It is the opposite of acting without thinking, often described as impulsivity. Finally, self-control has an attitudinal component that involves grit, or perseverance in the face of substantial obstacles (Duckworth, Gendler, & Gross, 2014).

Okay, I'm slicing the SEL pie into three broad categories—comprehension, execution, and self-control. There are a couple of things you should be aware of. First, as you've probably surmised by now, others cut the pie differently. Second, although this way of thinking about what SEL includes is quite broad, it does not easily accommodate student beliefs and attitudes. Some may object that this omits things like growth mind-set, self-efficacy, and other important ways children have of understanding the world that affect their manner of engaging it. Work on areas like growth mind-sets (Dweck, 2006) has been tremendously valuable, and my hope is that the guidance offered in this book about assessing comprehension, execution, and self-control are applicable to assessing adjacent beliefs, attitudes, dispositions, and skills that are not strictly in the universe of SEL skills, as defined here.

Deciding What SEL Skills Matter Most

The next step is to bring together the team that will develop an operational definition of SEL, likely in a sequence of meetings, and, using the chosen SEL model as an anchor and a menu, to identify the SEL skills that matter most. The guiding question of these conversations is some version of, "If we were able to nurture a handful of social and emotional skills in all our students, what would make the biggest difference?" By biggest difference, I mean both the biggest difference in advancing the district's mission, and, more broadly, in supporting children's ability to participate in and contribute to classroom life, to learn, and to connect with peers.

Start with your preferred model. Nominate the skills in that model that are most important, keeping in mind local priorities—articulated, for example, in the school's strategic plan, mission statement, or statement of values (and state guidelines and standards, if applicable). For each skill that is nominated, define it in a clear and specific way. Then categorize each skill as comprehension, execution, or self-control. Record all of your decisions on the worksheet presented in Table 1.1.

Imagine, for example, a district whose mission is to create engaged and socially responsible citizens prepared for an increasingly diverse and interdependent workforce. The group charged with identifying priority social and emotional skills, using the CASEL model as their anchor and menu, identifies several skills they believe are critical to achieving that mission, including social perspective-taking, social problem-solving, and social engagement. These skills are also in the district's state's standards. In the discussions, the group works to specify an operational definition for each. They deliberate and decide that perspective-taking means being able to infer another person's intentions and beliefs. They decide that problem-solving means being able to generate solutions to socially challenging problems, evaluate the likely consequences of each, and select the best solution. They decide that social engagement means assertiveness and positive social initiative during interpersonal and collaborative tasks. The group records these decisions on the worksheet in Table 1.1. For each skill, they write the reason it is important by referring to the district's mission statement.

TABLE 1.1 Defining SEL Worksheet

In our district, we define social and emotional competence overall as:

_____

We value social and emotional learning because: _____

_____

#	SPECIFIC SKILL	WHY IT MATTERS TO US	CATEGORY
			❏ Comprehension ❏ Execution ❏ Self-Control
			❏ Comprehension ❏ Execution ❏ Self-Control
			❏ Comprehension ❏ Execution ❏ Self-Control
			❏ Comprehension ❏ Execution ❏ Self-Control
			❏ Comprehension ❏ Execution ❏ Self-Control
			❏ Comprehension ❏ Execution ❏ Self-Control

Available to download at www.wwnorton.com/rd/mckown

Next, the group categorizes each of these three skills in terms of comprehension, execution, and self-control. On reflection, they determine that perspective-taking involves mainly a thinking process—inferring another person's intentions or beliefs. They therefore categorize perspective-taking as a comprehension skill. They deliberate over problem-solving, noting that in solving a problem there are mental components such as thinking of possible solutions and evaluating the consequences of an action, and behavioral components, such as enacting a solution. In reviewing their operational definition, they note that the skills described (generating solutions, evaluating their consequences, and selecting the best solution) are largely mental processes, and so they categorize them as comprehension. They deliberate over assertiveness and decide that social initiative during interpersonal and collaborative involves observable behavior and so categorize it as execution. They record these decisions on the worksheet in Table 1.1.

The group continues the process of identifying the most important skills and classifying each in to a broad category (comprehension, execution, and self-control). All decisions are recorded on the worksheet in Table 1.1. They aspire to create a list of skills that is clear to an outsider who has not been part of the conversation.

Finalizing Your Definition

There is a high likelihood that these conversations, if they are going well, will, at some point, have an in-the-weeds feel, meaning that everyone feels a little confused about what the main skills of interest are, perhaps mixed with differences of opinion about what is most important. I would venture to say that until district personnel have experienced murkiness and friction and worked their way through to clarity, the process is not complete. The struggle is an important part of coming to clarity and committing, together, to what will be the district's focus. Having a good model to anchor the discussions will help but won't prevent all struggle. To get to a sufficient level of struggle and therefore clarity and commitment will likely require regularly convening the team in a disciplined and ongoing process of exploration.

After going through the struggle and coming to clarity and consensus, the next step will be for district leadership to approve the definition. Some districts may opt for a public comment period, in which parents and other community members can learn about, respond to, and provide input on the working definition. After public comment, final revision, and approval, the definition of SEL that will be the district's focus should be communicated early and often to all staff and to the community. The definition will serve as one of two critical steps needed to wisely select the right assessment and engage in a useful process of reviewing the assessment data. The second critical step, coming to clarity on your assessment goals, is the focus of Chapter 2.

Why Assess
Children's SEL?

Even if you are fascinated, as I am, by children's understanding of the social world, that alone is not enough justification for the time and expense involved in assessing children's SEL. On the other hand, regardless of your level of interest in children's SEL, if you are an educator, periodically assessing all students' SEL skills can be a potent means to focus your instruction and improve student outcomes. If you've gone to the considerable trouble of defining what you mean by SEL, it probably means you already have some goal in mind for assessing and addressing this important dimension of children's development. Still, because there are many different reasons you might go about assessing student social and emotional skills, it is important to be clear about and declare which assessment goals you are (and are not) going to pursue. Although this may seem like a rather esoteric consideration, it has real-world consequences. If Chapter 1 was about clarifying *what* you're going to assess, Chapter 2 is about clarifying *why* you will assess it.

Problems That SEL Assessment Helps Solve

Let's talk about some of the most common reasons to undertake assessment and look at the possibilities and pitfalls that accompany each of these goals. At press time, in my opinion, the field of SEL assessment is not yet ready to achieve all these goals, but I list them here because they are common reasons educators might consider assessing student SEL:

- *Formative assessment*—to measure student strengths and needs for the purposes of modifying teaching to enhance student learning
- *Summative assessment*—to measure student skill acquisition at the end of an instructional period
- *Progress monitoring*—to measure skills repeatedly during instruction for tracking skill acquisition and student response to intervention
- *Program evaluation*—to measure the amount of skill acquired by groups of students who have been exposed to an instructional program or intervention
- *Continuous improvement/low-stakes accountability*—to identify opportunities for improvement and to use the findings to develop better ways to support teacher effectiveness and student success
- *Screening*—to classify student risk for a condition or disorder for which they will benefit from intervention or therapeutic support

- *Diagnosis*—to determine whether a child meets diagnostic criteria for a disorder or disability, often for the purposes of special education placement
- *High-stakes accountability*—to use assessment data to make inferences about the performance of teachers, principals, and others, and potentially to make decisions about hiring, firing, personnel compensation, and school funding

Undoubtedly, it is possible to describe other assessment goals, and reasonable people may disagree about the exact distinction between these assessment goals. In addition, it is likely that there is some overlap between these goals. Nevertheless, they provide helpful guideposts for our exploration of assessment goals. To that end, we'll explore getting to goal clarity next. You'll find that I often focus on formative assessment. This is because, in my experience, educators most commonly want to assess SEL to inform teaching and learning, and existing SEL assessments are arguably most well suited to supporting that goal. Most are not well suited to screening, diagnosis, or high-stakes accountability.

The Consequences of Clarity (and Lack Thereof)

After you work out what parts of SEL you think are most important, but before you select an assessment, there are good reasons to be clear about your goals. This is practical—if you have a clear goal in mind, you're more likely to achieve it. A clear goal facilitates communication about the SEL assessment initiative to audiences who will be affected by it. A clear goal also lays the groundwork for selecting an assessment that is valid for achieving your specific goal, reducing the odds of unintended negative consequences. It's only assessment, you say. What's the big deal? Well, there is some truth to that. However, I wouldn't be so passionate about assessment if I didn't think it could have an impact on the world. And if that is true, then there is the possibility that some of the impact of assessment could be negative.

Much of the risk that can come from student SEL assessment arises from a lack of clear goals in undertaking the assessment. Imagine, for example, a district team that is excited about supporting student SEL and has decided to undertake assessment. So far, so good. But they haven't really defined why they want to do this assessment. They just have a broad commitment to assessing the things they care about. Their approach to SEL assessments is, "Assess now, ask questions later." They go ahead and collect teacher report and direct assessments of student skills in October. Now they have a tremendous amount of information about their students.

Because no one is clear about the goals of assessment, a couple of things are likely to happen. First, a few parents may catch wind that their children's SEL is going to be assessed and demand to know what is going on and why. Without a clearly defined goal, it's hard to answer those questions (see Chapter 4 for more on engaging parents as partners). Second, all the educators in the system will, at best, wonder what to do with the assessment data. More likely, the data will be roundly ignored, and so all the time and expense of assessing students will have gone to waste. Third, teachers, already under the gun, may be concerned that the test scores will be used to evaluate their performance; likewise, principals may wonder if their schools will be judged on their students' social and emotional skill level. Fourth, well-meaning and passionate members of the team may use the assessment data in ways that pose undue risk, such as diagnosing children using assessment data that are not valid for the purposes of rendering a diagnosis. In sum, when assessment without clear goals is undertaken, the best-case scenario is that something good will accidentally happen. More often, nothing will happen. Neither is great. The worst-case scenario is that the data will be used inappropriately and have a negative impact.

Contrast that school district with another district whose team is equally passionate about SEL, and who spend time and energy getting really clear about why they want to assess these skills. In this district, for example, they have been using a well-regarded SEL program for several years. The team suspect that they could use the lesson plans and SEL strategies in a more focused way to build on student strengths and address student needs. However, they do not yet have a way to get a clear snapshot of student strengths and needs, making it difficult to differentiate instruction in a way that might have a greater impact. It is as if they were charged with implementing an evidence-based math curriculum but did not have any formal information about student math skills. Where should they start? What should they emphasize? What skills are well developed and so represent a foundation? What skills need further development?

From this situation, district leadership, with input from principals and teachers, has identified formative assessment as a critical SEL assessment goal. They will assess in the fall, and assessment results will be shared in grade-level team meetings. Professional development will be provided to support teachers in understanding and using the assessment data to understand their students and decide how, based on what they learn, they can best approach the task of teaching their students the skills they need to be successful in school and life (see Chapter 5 for more on effective data use practices). Furthermore, they affirmatively decide they will not use the assessment to evaluate teachers or schools. Nor will they use assessment for program evaluation, diagnosis, or continuous improvement. They communicate these goals early, often, and clearly to teachers and other educators and to the parent community.

The intentional way this district has gone about defining the goals of assessment prevents, or at least ameliorates, the kinds of problems facing the first district. Here, everyone understands the purpose of the assessment. They understand what is expected of them and what they will get in return. Systems are established for the effective use of the assessment data. Teachers get curious, even excited, about learning more about their students' strengths and needs. No one is worried that the results will be used against them. Parents are largely put at ease by the goal clarity, and it is easier for district leadership and everyone else to address any remaining parent concerns as all can speak clearly to why assessment is being undertaken and what it will and will not be used for. After assessment is completed, the assessment data are used in discussions about students, and so there is a clear payoff for the investment of time and resources required to do the assessment. Teaching staff use what they learn to modify their use of the

SEL curriculum and, if all goes well, this increases the impact of their work with students.

I recognize that this study in contrasts is a little exaggerated. Some districts whose leadership doesn't clarify their goals clearly will nevertheless discover wonderful uses for the data. Others who rigorously clarify their goals may find that the data nevertheless go unused. However, the odds of success are greatly increased with goal clarity, and I do believe that any school system contemplating SEL assessment to improve programs and student outcomes will be well served by spending the time and effort required to answer the question of why they are going to assess students. The clearer the answer, the more likely that all involved will believe in and benefit from SEL assessment.

Getting to Clarity

If you agree with the premise of this chapter that clear assessment goals are important to facilitate success, promote effective communication, maximize benefit, and minimize risk, you might be asking yourself what is required to get to goal clarity. As was the case with defining SEL, defining your goal, if you are doing it right, will be challenging and will require hard work and the engagement of multiple constituencies. So, unfortunately, there is no easy answer to how to get there. Having said that, I suspect that for most educators going to the trouble of assessing student SEL, there are two main resources for getting clear about the reasons for assessment.

Let's call the first resource top-down or executive inspiration. Someone in the district's leadership—the superintendent or a cabinet member—has a strong belief that SEL assessment would help to advance practice and student outcomes. Perhaps student SEL is a priority in the district's strategic plan or state standards, or figures prominently in the mission or district values statements. Let's call the second resource bottom-up or grassroots inspiration. In this case, classroom teachers come to recognize that their teaching, and their students' outcomes, would benefit from a better assessment of student SEL skills. Perhaps, for example, teachers are noticing the impact of social and emotional skills on students' ability to participate effectively in collaborative group work. They would like to assess and address the SEL skills that will contribute to successful collaboration.

Both sources of inspiration are important first steps toward clarity. I use the word "inspiration" because, in my experience, most people come to a general idea of what might make life better by a gut feeling that is not particularly focused, and I assume this is the case most of the time when educators begin to contemplate SEL assessment. Think of the first inspiration as a general instinct that SEL assessment might make a difference. That's a great start, but it is usually not the clearest impulse in the world. The beautiful thing about inspiration is that, unfocused though it may be, it contains all the energy needed to impel the inspired toward clarity, if it is channeled well.

The task, then, is to channel inspiration. That is a leadership exercise. The group in Chapter 1 that was empowered to clarify what student SEL skills matter most might get pressed into service now. The group's charge is to develop and articulate a clear SEL assessment goal. Doing so requires the group to answer the question, "What do we want to accomplish by assessing student social and emotional learning?" Three main sources can help answer that question: the group members themselves, members of district leadership, and teaching staff. Others may be included on this list, such as school counselors. All these groups represent important resources for understanding the varied goals educators in a district might pursue by assessing student SEL. In most cases, the group leading the goal clarification effort will solicit and take seriously the input from these sources. The alternative to seeking input is to make an executive decision. In some circumstances, that may be fine, but pursuing early input from those who will be affected by assessment increases the odds that all will be, at a minimum, singing from the same sheet.

As someone interested in the challenge of asking questions productively, I recognize that there are any number of ways to ask this question that will quickly yield an overwhelming set of conflicting answers. I'm generally a believer in open-ended questions. But in this case, if the group working on goal clarification asks the broad question, "What do we want to accomplish by assessing student SEL?," such a purely grassroots approach creates a vast decision space into which imaginative respondents might dream up all kinds of goals. What might result under these conditions is a crazy quilt of ideas, some of which might not fit together easily (such as screening and identification and formative assessment). This may create problems later when the district opts to pursue one of these goals over others, leaving some constituents disengaged because they feel ignored.

To prevent this problem while still meaningfully obtaining input from different constituents requires a narrowing of the decision space using a judicious combination of executive and grassroots approaches. This begins with one of two executive decision frames. One is to identify, at the district cabinet level, a limited number of goals, all of which would be productive for teaching and learning and ask people to respond to those options. What goals do they like and why? Which do they dislike? A second, if there is a strong reason to define the goal before seeking input, is to draft the goal along with district cabinet members and ask other constituents what they think. What do they like about the goal? What do they dislike? How might they improve it? Either method will yield meaningful information from those whose lives would be affected by assessing student SEL—information that can help in choosing a final assessment goal.

The team charged with planning the SEL assessment initiative should carefully consider which constituents will share input. I recommend seeking input from all constituents who may be affected by or benefit from SEL assessment data. This will almost surely include district leadership, principals, and classroom teachers. It will likely include school counselors, social workers, and psychologists. It may also include staff who will be involved in implementing assessment processes, including IT staff, and whoever at the school level will be responsible for assessment administration.

After collecting this information, the team working on assessment goal clarification will summarize their findings and present them to district decision makers to consider and finalize. This report should include a clear statement of what the goal of SEL student assessment is and is not. For example, it might conclude that student SEL assessment will be undertaken for the purposes of informing instruction, and monitoring SEL skill development. It might also conclude that student SEL assessment will not be used for diagnosis, placement in special education, teacher evaluation, or high stakes accountability. These clear statements will help ensure that all have a very clear understanding of the purposes of assessment. This will aid communication and increase the odds that the assessment data will be used for focused and productive purposes.

Once the goal is clarified and the recommendation made, deliberated over, and approved, the next task is communicating that goal. The final goal should be communicated to principals, teachers, and the parent community to orient these constituents to the reason you are going to undertake the task of assessing student SEL.

So now you've defined what you mean by SEL. You've done some hard work to clarify goals. Now it's time to select the right tool for the job. That's the focus of Chapter 3.

Selecting the Right Tool for the Job

If you took the trouble to read Chapters 1 and 2, please skip the rest of this paragraph. To those of you who are still reading this paragraph, I suspect, dear reader, that you skipped Chapters 1 and 2, perhaps because you think defining SEL and clarifying your goals are not important or that you've already got it nailed. You wanted to get to the good stuff. Understandable. Cake is surely tastier than veggies, and of course you should use this volume in the way you see fit. Eat dessert first, if you like. But please bear this in mind: regardless of its technical merit, an assessment tool is a dumb instrument, like a scalpel. To use it to its greatest effect requires thoughtful preparation and no small commitment of sweat equity. So, dear reader, take a deep breath, and before you go on, take at least a minute to decide whether you really want to wield the scalpel before deciding exactly where to operate.

You have arrived at one of the most consequential points in the whole process—selecting the specific tool you will use to assess the dimensions of SEL you care about to achieve the goals that are important to you. At press time, the number of options for assessing SEL was modest but rapidly growing. The field is new enough, and the assessment options scattered across enough different organizations, that it takes some sleuthing to find out what's possible. In this chapter, we'll talk about the kinds of assessments that are available for assessing children's SEL, and the goals each assessment approach is best suited to advancing. We'll suggest ways to identify candidate assessments, aided by a worksheet. We'll also discuss, mostly in nontechnical terms, the things to look for to determine which of your candidate assessments is the right tool for the job.

Measures for Different Assessment Goals

Several kinds of social and emotional assessment methods are available to those interested in assessing children's SEL, summarized in Table 3.1a and Table 3.1b. Self-report involves children reporting the frequency with which they engage in specific behaviors or their level of agreement with statements about their social and emotional skills. Typically, students are asked to rate several skills on a four- or five-point scale. Rating scales involve an adult, usually a teacher, rating the frequency with which a child engages in behaviors reflecting defined social and emotional skills. Observation involves recording behavior, often the frequency or presence of observed behaviors during a succession of time intervals. Direct behavior ratings are a hybrid of rating scales and observation in which a teacher rates the extent to which a child engaged in a small number of clearly defined behaviors during a specified observation period. Peer nomination involves children rating or nominating who they prefer or who engages in specific behaviors. Direct assessment involves children demonstrating their social and emotional skills through their response to challenging social and emotional tasks.

As you can see in Table 3.1a and Table 3.1b, each assessment method is better suited to measuring some dimensions of SEL than others. Reasonable people may disagree with this assessment of the strengths and limitations of each method, and their best use. I am certain that a creative person, for example, might find a terrific way to use direct behavior ratings (DBRs) for program evaluation, or incorporate observation into multitiered systems of support (MTSS), which involves data-based decision making about the level of instructional support children need. In addition, the astute reader will note that I only included four ways assessments can be used—formative assessment, program evaluation, continuous improvement, and MTSS. Yet, as we have discussed, there are other goals one might wish to use SEL assessment to advance. I included these goals because, in my view, they are the goals for which the most widely available SEL assessments are currently suitable.

The table reflects my opinion about the strengths, limitations, and reasonable uses of some of the most widely available methods of assessing

TABLE 3.1A Methods of Assessing Social Emotional Skills

METHOD	DESCRIPTION	GOOD FOR	LIMITATIONS
Teacher Report	Teachers rate the frequency with which students engage in behaviors reflecting social and emotional skill or problem behaviors.	Efficient assessment of student behavioral skills.	Teachers may use rating scales differently. Best for observable behaviors (such as aggression). Not as good for less visible skills.
Observation	Teachers (or others) observe children and rate the frequency of observed behavior, or rate whether behaviors occurred during discreet intervals.	Assessing high frequency and highly observable behaviors.	Difficult to achieve good inter-rater agreement without a lot of training. May miss low-frequency, high-impact behaviors (e.g., helping a friend; biting).
Direct Behavior Ratings	After a defined observation period, teacher records the percentage of the time target students engaged in a few of well-defined behaviors.	Efficient assessment of student behavioral skills. Tracking behavior change over time.	Focus on very small number of target behaviors may not do justice to the child's broader repertoire of skills.
Direct Assessment	Students demonstrate their skill level by solving challenging problems that reflect social and emotional skill.	Assessing "comprehension," the less visible mental skills children use in social encounters—like recognizing others' feelings, and thinking through social challenges.	Measures thinking skills, not behavior.
Self-Report	Students complete questionnaires in which they read statements about themselves and rate how true the statements are or how often what the statement describes is true.	Assessing students' perceptions of their skills, attitudes, and mindsets. Also good for assessing student perception of the climate.	Students may not be willing or able to accurately assess their skill level.
Peer Nomination	Children nominate classmates who display selected behaviors.	Assessing peer-rated social emotional execution.	Acceptability to community. Technical complexity.

TABLE 3.1B

METHOD	DESCRIPTION	ASSESSMENT GOAL			
		FA	PE	CI	MTSS
Teacher Report	Teachers rate the frequency with which students engage in behaviors reflecting social and emotional skill or problem behaviors.	✓✓	✓	✓	✓✓
Observation	Teachers (or others) observe children and rate the frequency of observed behavior, or rate whether behaviors occurred during discreet intervals.	✓	✓		
Direct Behavior Ratings	After a defined observation period, teacher records the percentage of the time target students engaged in a few of well-defined behaviors.	✓			✓✓
Direct Assessment	Students demonstrate their skill level by solving challenging problems that reflect social and emotional skill.	✓✓	✓	✓	✓
Self-Report	Students complete questionnaires in which they read statements about themselves and rate how true the statements are or how often what the statement describes is true.	✓✓	✓	✓	
Peer Nomination	Children nominate classmates who display selected behaviors.	✓	✓		✓

NOTE: FA=Formative Assessment; PE=Program Evaluation; CI=Continuous Improvement; MTSS=Multi-Tiered Systems of Support.

children's social and emotional learning. I invite you to use it as a starting point for coming to your own judgments about SEL assessment, rather than viewing it as a definitive statement of fact.

Matching What You Want to Measure With Your Method

Let's revisit the different dimensions of social and emotional learning, described in Chapter 1, and review the suitability of different methods for assessing those dimensions.

Comprehension

Let's start with social and emotional comprehension. Social-emotional comprehension poses challenges that call for methods suited to its measurement. In contrast to social and emotional execution, by definition, social and emotional comprehension involves mental events that are not clearly visible to the outside world. This includes things like understanding what others are feeling, being able to see things from another person's point of view, knowing when an interpersonal problem arises, and having ideas about how to resolve social problems. The more skillfully children pick up social cues and think through social problems, the more likely they are to enjoy successful interactions and positive peer relationships.

It is true that some behaviors can give observers clues about comprehension skills—for example, a child might say something that reveals an understanding of another person's feelings or intentions, allowing an observer to infer the child's perspective-taking skill level. However, unlike execution, which expresses itself in observable action, comprehension exists in the mind and requires a much higher level of inference for observers to make an accurate appraisal. Social and emotional comprehension is, in that sense, akin to reading skills. Yes, a teacher could assess children's reading skills using a teacher questionnaire, but direct assessments of reading skills are more likely to yield a useful appraisal of a child's ability to decode words, read fluently, and understand what he reads. Similarly, direct social and emotional assessment is well suited to assessing social and emotional comprehension. With direct assessment, for example, a child can demonstrate how well she can read others' emotions by looking at pictures and saying what the people feel, or demonstrate social problem-solving skills by responding to hypothetical problem situations. This provides a direct window into social and emotional comprehension that avoids some of the limitations of other methods.

Many social and emotional skills take place largely or exclusively between children's ears and are therefore well suited to direct assessment. Children's understanding of others' emotions, as reflected in their ability to read facial expressions; children's understanding of others' beliefs or intentions; children's social goals and attributions about the causes of others' behavior; children's preferred strategies for solving social problems; children's emotion regulation knowledge—these are all examples of important social and emotional skills that may be difficult to ascertain from observation, but may be well suited to direct assessment.

Execution

In contrast to comprehension, social and emotional execution involves observable behaviors. These include actions children take to connect positively with others, like inviting peers into conversations, taking turns, entering ongoing activities appropriately, compromising, and helping others in distress. These are just some examples of the kinds of things children do that contribute to successful interactions, positive peer relationships, and a healthy classroom climate.

Some forms of assessment are better suited to measuring observable behaviors than others. Rating scales, behavioral observation, DBRs, and peer nominations are well suited to assessing observed behaviors. Well-validated rating scales are available and can yield reliable scores that are valid for understanding children's behavioral strengths and needs. They can pose something of a burden on teachers who must complete many items for many children. Behavioral observation is arguably the most difficult to execute with sufficient reliability and validity. Despite the seeming simplicity of this assessment approach, the time and effort required to collect reliable observation data valid for understanding student SEL skills is, in most cases, prohibitive. Direct behavior ratings are both feasible and probably best suited for monitoring behavioral progress. Peer nominations can also yield helpful assessments, from the point of view of classmates, of the extent to which children engage in positive and aversive behaviors.

Self-Control

Self-control includes specific thinking skills such as cognitive and emotion regulation, and their behavioral expression. This includes things like being able to wait for something desirable, being able to tolerate frustration and disappointment, knowing how to stay calm when upset, being able to sit still and pay attention, and being able to refrain from impulsive actions such as blurting out answers in class. These examples include a combination of mental skills (such as emotion regulation) and behavioral skills (refraining from impulsivity).

The mental dimensions of self-control may be measured through direct assessment and, in some cases, self-report. For example, direct assessments have been developed that measure higher-order cognitive skills called executive functions (Obradovic, Sulik, Finch, & Tirado-Strayer, 2018). These include the abilities to inhibit responses, to flexibly apply different problem-solving rules, and to hold information in short-term memory and manipulate that information. Although these skills may seem somewhat esoteric, a substantial body of research suggests that they are related to academic and social outcomes. Furthermore, these are mental processes that are difficult to see and therefore are not ideally suited to observational or rating-scale strategies. In addition, children (and adults!) may be unaware of their working memory capacity, rendering self-reported skills of limited utility. It seems clear that for these skills, direct assessment is the right tool for the job.

Behaviors reflecting the absence of self-control are quite visible to the observer. As a result, they may be well and accurately measured through observation, rating scales, or other observational strategies. For example, rating scales that include items designed to measure impulsivity capture behavioral dysregulation. These scales will ask teachers to indicate how frequently children engage in specific behaviors, such as, "Acts without thinking." In addition, self-control may be reflected in beliefs and attitudes about the self. The concept of grit, for example, defined as "perseverance and passion for long-term goals" (Duckworth, Peterson, Matthews, & Kelly, 2007, p. 1087), is a component of self-control that is often measured with self-report. Therefore, depending on the purpose of assessment and what dimension of self-control is measured, self-report may be appropriate.

The discussion so far has made little mention of peer nomination as a tactic for assessing social and emotional skills. With peer nomination, children nominate or rate peers who they prefer, or who engage in positive or aversive behaviors. Peer nomination strategies can provide important insights about peer acceptance and social and emotional execution. However, there are two substantial barriers to using peer nomination for many school districts. First, many bristle at the idea of having children rate one another. Second, collecting, scoring, and interpreting peer nomination data is not a straightforward process. Interested districts can find peer nomination assessments, and use them to good effect, but it will require a careful consideration of the acceptability of this method and the resources available to implement it and to interpret the data.

Identifying Candidate Assessments

Your job at this point is to identify candidate assessment tools. Up until very recently, the only resources available for learning about SEL assessment tools were internet searches, advertisements, and word of mouth. There is nothing wrong with these approaches, but they have a disadvantage: it is very difficult to come even close to identifying all of assessment candidates that might be useful to you. Instead of a universe of alternatives from which you may select the best fit, you'll generally be exposed to options you stumble on while searching the internet or talking to a trusted colleague. Either route will often lead you to products from companies with enough resources to create beautiful marketing materials. Using this method, you may not learn about harder to find options that are a potentially better fit for your needs.

Two new resources should help alleviate this problem and give you a better sense of the full range of SEL assessment options. The RAND Corporation has developed an online catalog of social and emotional assessments that includes descriptions of a broad range of assessment tools, including information about what they measure and their technical properties. In addition, CASEL has developed an online assessment guide. Like the RAND repository, the CASEL guide includes a catalog of assessments that meet CASEL quality standards, and includes information about what each assessment is for, what its technical properties are, administration information, score reporting, cost, and what developer support you can expect. CASEL is also developing a document that offers guidance about appropriate use. These resources should greatly help anyone who is interested in understanding the range of SEL assessment tools identify a broad range of assessment options.

The next step for the team leading the SEL assessment initiative is to select candidate assessment tools that assess what you identified as the most important SEL skills (see Chapter 1) to achieve your most pressing goals (see Chapter 2). Here's how to use what you've done so far to facilitate this process: First, go back to the worksheet in Table 1.1. Transfer the skills you identified from Chapter 1 and your categorization of each as either comprehension, execution, or self-control to the first two columns of the worksheet in Table 3.2 (find this worksheet at the end of this chapter). In the third column, check the box next to the method best suited to assessing that skill. Keep in mind, as we have discussed in this chapter, in general, comprehension is best assessed with direct assessments; execution is best assessed with teacher report or DBRs; self-control is best assessed with direct assessment or teacher ratings, and sometimes self-report.

Once you have completed the first three columns of the worksheet in Table 3.2, you are ready to identify candidate assessments. Here is where the RAND repository and CASEL guide are particularly useful. Keeping in mind what you want to assess, what kind of skill it is (comprehension, execution, or self-control), and the type of assessment you want to use, review the repository and guide to identify assessment candidates that are the best fit. For each skill, identify at least one candidate assessment.

Now that you've identified candidate assessments, it's time to evaluate their strengths and limitations to determine which assessment is best suited to assessing what you want to measure to achieve your assessment goals.

That involves reviewing the technical properties of the assessment to make sure it's up to the task. The next section walks you through the qualities to look for in an assessment.

Evaluating the Candidates: A Consumer's Guide to Psychometrics

Psychometrics refers broadly to the science of measuring mental processes. The field is vast and, although seemingly arcane, incredibly important for anyone who is interesting in measuring things like SEL. The good news is that you don't need to be a measurement scientist to be a good consumer of assessments. What you need is an understanding of what to look for to understand the quality of an assessment and, sometimes, a measurement expert to help double-check that your evaluation of a measurement system's technical qualities, and its suitability for the inferences you plan to make from the assessment scores, are reasonable. There are three main technical properties to consider when reviewing the suitability of an assessment: reliability, validity, and measurement equivalence.

Reliability

Reliability refers to the reproducibility of the scores. A reliable score is one that consistently produces the same or a very similar score when measuring something. Let's step out of the less tangible arena of SEL and think about the reliability of a well-understood score—your height. The instrument used to measure height is commonly some form of measuring stick. Now, if that stick is made of a very hard metal and is used to measure height in the same manner every time, you should get a similar result each time. I'm about 6'3" tall. A reliable measuring system will yield the same score each time. One can imagine a less reliable method of measuring height—using a rubber measuring stick or a highly elastic string, for example. What I might learn about my height from these imperfect instruments depends on how much error variability is introduced by the lack of assessment reliability. It's not that the less reliable methods are useless—it's just that they introduce a level of uncertainty that permits an estimated range more than a precise number. I might learn, for example, that there's a 95% chance that my height is somewhere between 5'11" and 6'5". The higher the reliability of the score, the smaller that range will be.

Because they measure complex and often invisible processes that cannot be directly measured in the way that height can, all educational, behavioral, and psychological assessments include some amount of error, by which I mean they don't measure with perfect reliability. Reliability is usually judged in terms of consistency of scores across items on the assessment, assessment occasions, and raters.

Consistency across items—or internal consistency reliability—refers to the extent to which respondents with a skill level in the assessed content area tend to perform consistently across items with similar difficulty levels that make up the overall score. Let's say an assessment is designed to assess children's ability to recognize others' emotions from their facial expressions. For the assessment, children look at pictures and indicate what each person is feeling. If the assessment is internally consistent, children should perform similarly across comparably difficult items that make up the total score. High internal consistency means the child's true skill level is well and precisely estimated by the score. Low internal consistency means that the child's true skill level is not precisely estimated by the score. It can also mean the assessment is measuring more than one thing—the apples and oranges problem.

Consistency across time—or test-retest reliability—refers to the extent to which respondents tend to achieve a similar score when they are assessed more than once. Back to the ruler example: good test-retest reliability means that repeated measures of my height yield a very similar score (6′3″ish). Similarly, academic, behavioral, and psychological assessments should yield similar scores on repeated measurement. It is important to note, however, that unlike height, we expect behavior, skills, and knowledge to change over relatively short periods of time. As a result, it is not always necessary for an assessment to have extremely high test-retest reliability, particularly over long time intervals during which we expect children's skills to develop at different rates. Still, it is an important criterion for you to consider as you evaluate your assessment options.

Consistency across raters—or inter-rater reliability—refers to the extent to which two people give the same score to a sample of behavior, such as a response to an assessment item or an observed behavior. Inter-rater reliability is important because it quantifies the extent to which a score arising from the judgment of raters reflects the thing they are observing and not the idiosyncratic judgments of the raters. Inter-rater reliability is a particularly important consideration for assessments that require a rater to make a judgment when scoring, and is commonly reported to judge the reliability of observation systems. For example, DBRs require teachers to estimate the percentage of time a student was engaged in specific behaviors over a brief interval.

There are other kinds of reliability, but the first two are the most commonly reported and, arguably, the two most important. Each score that an assessment gives you will have an associated internal consistency reliability and test-retest reliability that you can research and use to evaluate the suitability of candidate assessments. And the good news is that we have good methods of quantifying the reliability of a score in ways that make it relatively easy to evaluate the level of certainty one can attribute to a score. Assessment developers can (and should) report score reliabilities in their technical manuals. Reliability scores range from 0 to 1, where 0 means not at all reliable and 1 means perfectly reliable. There is no hard and fast rule about what is reliable enough.

Having said that, my read of convention is that an internal consistency reliability of .70 may be good enough for reporting group level performance— aggregated at the classroom level or above—but is not good enough to assess individual student strengths and needs for any reason, particularly for high-stakes decision. That is because with a reliability of .70, a child's score on an assessment may be quite different from one administration to another, increasing the chances that you will come to an incorrect, and potentially harmful, conclusion about a child from the assessment's scores. A child, for example, may achieve a very low score that underestimates her actual skill levels, which could easily lead to an erroneous conclusion about that student. A reliability of .80 may be good enough to evaluate individual student strengths and needs, but not to make high-stakes decisions, including diagnosis or placement in special education services. If interpreted well, scores with this level of reliability may help provide formative information educators can use to tune instruction in a way that builds on the student's strengths and addresses her needs. A reliability of at least .90 is required for more high-stakes decision making. Test-retest reliabilities can be a little lower, particularly if the interval between testing occasions is longer than two weeks. Inter-rater reliabilities are a bit of a different animal, and because they are not relevant to many assessment types, I won't go into detail here. Regardless of the kind or level of score reliability, however, it is important to note that the appropriateness of using assessment scores to achieve a specific goal depends on other factors in addition to reliability.

Validity

The second attribute to look at is validity, which refers to the extent to which the assessment measures what it was designed to measure. It also refers to evidence that the assessment can be used for a defined purpose. Don't confuse reliability and validity. A perfectly reliable assessment can be totally invalid. Our tempered steel measuring stick is very reliable, but it is not at all valid for measuring temperature. It is, however, valid for measuring height. Like our measuring stick, all assessments can only be valid for a limited range of purposes. Test makers use a lot of strategies to evaluate a test's validity, and some can be quite technical. For consumers of SEL assessments, I would encourage you to examine three kinds of evidence of validity.

First is face validity. This is the most superficial form of validity and refers to the extent to which the assessment content looks on its surface like it measures what it's designed to measure. This is the most accessible form of validity because it requires little technical expertise. But face validity alone is not enough to determine whether your candidate assessment will serve you well.

Second is criterion-related validity. This refers to the extent to which scores on the assessment in question are correlated with scores on other assessments of things that we would expect to be related to the assessment's content. In the case of SEL assessments, for example, a consistent association between performance on a direct assessment and a teacher rating scale focused on social behavior is evidence of criterion-related validity. This kind of validity evidence helps clarify the extent to which performance on the assessment is associated with other things that we care about.

One specific kind of criterion-related validity is called convergent and discriminant validity. An assessment that measures what it was designed to measure will yield a score that is more strongly correlated with scores from alternate assessments of the same thing (convergent validity) than with assessments of similar but distinct things (discriminant validity). For example, an assessment designed to measure children's understanding of others' emotions should be more strongly correlated with another assessment designed to measure emotion recognition than it is to an assessment designed to measure a similar but distinct skill such as social perspective-taking. Evidence of convergent and discriminant validity suggests that the assessment is measuring what it was designed to measure and not inadvertently measuring something else.

Third is structural validity. This refers to the extent to which the different dimensions measured by an assessment are associated with one another as predicted by theory. Imagine, for example, an achievement test designed to assesses reading speed, accuracy, and comprehension. If the theory underlying this assessment is that these three skill components of reading are partly distinct, evidence from validation research should demonstrate that scores from items reflecting each of the three skills will be more strongly related to one another than they are related to items reflecting other skills. Structural validity is typically determined with a statistical method called factor analysis.

Fourth is treatment validity. This refers to evidence that children's performance on the assessment changes when they participate in an effective intervention designed to influence what is measured. The first two forms of validity evidence will be included in the technical manual. This last form is often not available, but if it is, it can be helpful, particularly when you are interested in assessment to evaluate program impact.

Taking the measure of validity evidence. Validity evidence is not as straightforward as reliability metrics, but there are some guidelines for their interpretation. Criterion-related validity analyses will often consist of correlation coefficients that tell us how strong the relationship is between the SEL test score and other assessments (the criterion measures). Like reliability coefficients, correlation coefficients range from 0 to 1, with 0 meaning there is no relationship and 1 meaning, essentially, the two assessments measure the same thing. As with reliability, there is no hard and fast rule about what size of correlation is sufficient. What you want to see is that scores on the assessment you are considering are consistently related to scores on alternate measures of the same thing and less related to scores on assessments of different things. Coefficients in the .3 to .6 range and higher may be adequate. You'll need to weigh the totality of the evidence to feel confident that the assessment is valid for your purposes.

Treatment validity is established with evidence of an assessment's ability to detect intervention effects. At the broadest level, when the evidence suggests that students who participate in an SEL program do better on the assessment than comparable students who do not participate in the program, this provides evidence of treatment validity. A manual or independent research study might indicate that in a program evaluation that included an intervention group and a control group, students in the intervention group performed better after the intervention than children in the control group. The quality of the study, the magnitude of the difference between treatment and control groups, and other considerations give you important information. Overall, look for evidence that scores on an assessment improve more when children participate in a program designed to teach the skills assessed compared to children who do not. That reflects evidence of treatment validity.

Measurement equivalence. The American cultural tapestry is on display in its full glory perhaps nowhere more clearly than the schoolhouse, with students from different ethnic and cultural backgrounds, different home languages, and different socioeconomic backgrounds gathered together in common cause. As a result, any universal SEL assessment initiative will include children with widely divergent life experiences. This raises the important question of whether the same social and emotional skills are equally important for all students and the related question of whether any one assessment can be counted on to give us an equally reliable and valid set of scores summarizing a student's social and emotional skills. The broad term for the latter property of assessments is measurement equivalence.

Tempting but flawed ways to evaluate possible bias. On its surface, measurement equivalence may seem straightforward. It is not. One simple but incorrect, or at least highly error-prone, way to judge measurement equivalence is to look at the content of the assessment. Do the images and assessment content seem to be culturally relevant? It is surely a good thing for assessment developers to be mindful of this consideration, and it is possible that this will affect measurement equivalence. However, it is impossible to determine from the appearance of an assessment whether it measures what it is intended to measure equally well and in an unbiased fashion for all groups. An assessment that looks biased may function beautifully for all groups; another that appears to be culturally relevant, on the other hand, can fail sophisticated tests of measurement equivalence.

Another simple but incorrect way to assess measurement equivalence is to evaluate whether children from different groups achieve different average scores on the assessment, with the assumption that any mean difference is evidence of bias. Children from different groups may in fact differ in their average SEL skill level, and a mean difference on test scores might be an accurate reflection of those differences. This can raise problems, described below in the section on broader cultural considerations, but is not necessarily a reflection of a flawed assessment. Mean differences between groups reflects a technical flaw when children from different groups *with the same ability level* achieve different scores on the items or test. If that is happening, then mean differences between groups reflect test bias.

What's a better way? If these are wrong ways to assess measurement equivalence, what are the right ways? This brings us into some rather esoteric and technical material that is beyond the scope of this book. Here is a brief lay summary. There are two kinds of measurement equivalence that can and should be tested empirically. The first is item equivalence, typically evaluated using Rasch or item response theory methods. The question here is, do children from different groups who have the same skill level tend to get the same score on each item? If not, the item displays differential item functioning and may need to be revised or thrown out to ensure the overall test is unbiased.

The second is test score equivalence, typically assessed using confirmatory factor analysis methods. There are three particularly important kinds of test score equivalence. The first is *configural* invariance, which means that the tests measure the same things in all groups. (Back to our yard stick metaphor: does the yard stick measure length in all cases?) Next is *metric* invariance, which means that a one-point score difference means the same thing for children from different groups. (Does the difference between the tick marks on the yard stick mean the same thing for all groups?) And finally is *scalar* invariance, which means that children with the same skill level achieve the same score on the assessment. (Do children who are 5′3″ tall register as 5′3″ tall regardless of their group membership?) Ideally, an assessment will demonstrate configural, metric, and scalar invariance.

One challenge in the field of behavioral assessment is that assessment developers often do not test and report evidence of item or test score equivalence, so it is difficult to know whether an assessment is unbiased. A second challenge is that evidence of bias does not necessarily render an assessment useless. However, depending on the kind of nonequivalence, the uses and interpretations of the scores may be limited. For example, a test that exhibits evidence of configural and metric invariance, but some evidence of scalar non-invariance, can still be used. However, users should be cautious in interpreting mean group differences, as those differences may not reflect differences in skill level. In addition, scalar non-invariance may be remedied, for example, by creating separate norms for the groups in question.

Even with evidence of measurement equivalence, because SEL assessments may sometimes seem not to reflect a local community, some may argue for adapting assessment content to fit the local cultural context. Before you do this, be aware that if you modify rigorously validated and well-normed assessments, evidence of its technical properties is rendered null and void. You'll be starting with a new and unproven assessment tool that may in fact be more biased than the original, but with no way of knowing how well it works for anyone, or whether it works equally well for everyone. Don't throw out the proverbial baby with the bathwater.

My main message here is that measurement equivalence is a technically complex topic. Intuitive ways of assessing cultural relevance may be misleading. At the same time, rigorous tests of measurement equivalence are often not undertaken or reported by test makers, and so it is possible that you will not have the evidence you need to determine in a satisfactory way whether an assessment is equally good for all children, regardless of their sex, ethnicity, socioeconomic status, or other important group membership.

Brass Tacks: Selecting the Right Tool

Okay. So how do you choose from among the options? First, make sure the candidate assessments are designed to assess what you care about. Second, make sure the assessments are appropriate tools for achieving your assessment goals, based on evidence of score reliability and validity for your specific goals. Third, develop plans that ensure that SEL assessment benefits children from all communities. For every candidate assessment you have identified and documented in the worksheet shown in Table 3.2, record in evidence of reliability, validity, and measurement equivalence un the columns on strengths and weaknesses. You can then weigh these quality considerations along with cost and administration burden, to make your final choice.

As you may have gathered, evaluating the technical properties of an assessment is not always a straightforward matter. Anyone going through the process of reviewing assessment options would do well to include on the review team someone with the training and expertise to help interpret evidence about the assessments' technical merits. School psychologists, directors of assessment and accountability, and others in the district often have training in psychometrics appropriate to supporting your review of assessment quality. They should be called upon to help sort through evidence about reliability and validity, as well as provide their judgment about the appropriateness, given the assessment's technical merits, for assessing what you want to assess to achieve your goals.

This chapter has focused on how to choose the right SEL assessment, where the right assessment is the one that measures what you care about and has the right qualities and technical properties in light of your assessment goals. This implies, and it is in fact the case, that it is possible to choose the wrong tool for the job. It's worthwhile to spend a little time clarifying what it would mean to choose the wrong tool for the job and what the consequences might be.

The Wrong Tool for the Job

The first thing to know is that every assessment can be the wrong tool for the job. No assessment is appropriate for measuring all things or for meeting all possible assessment goals. Every assessment has strengths and weaknesses. This means that for every assessment, there are potential mismatches between what the assessment is designed to do, what the assessor is trying to assess, and what goals they are trying to achieve. At the same time, assessments are dumb. They don't know how you're going to use them, and they have no say in the matter. This means that it's up to the assessment developer to provide information that will permit the users to evaluate the fit between the assessment and the assessment target and goal. It also means it's up to you to be clear-minded in your judgments about the fit between the assessment itself, the target and goal of assessment, and the inferences and decisions you will make from the assessment data.

Any use of an assessment to achieve a goal for which it is not valid is what I've come to think of an "off-label" use of the assessment, like using a medication designed to treat one condition for a different condition. As is the case with medication, off-label assessment use carries risks. Anyone considering assessing student SEL needs to understand how an assessment can (and cannot) be used and to make sure that assessment is well suited to achieving their assessment goals. Each of the existing SEL assessment systems has a sweet spot, with some well-suited to formative assessment and others well suited to progress monitoring, for example. As you consider the options, make sure the assessment you choose is well-suited to achieving your assessment goal.

If you're not sure, ask the assessment developers to walk you through what this assessment is good at and what it's not good at. A key question to ask is, "For what purpose is your assessment valid?" They should provide clear and simple guidance about their assessments' strengths and weaknesses, so you can know what it can be used for, and what constitutes off-label use. Ask what evidence they have to support their claims about the assessments' strengths and needs. The best assessment developers will give you an honest appraisal of what their assessment system can and can't do, and they can back up their claims with evidence.

Off-label use is not forbidden, and in some cases might be a good idea. Think of it in medical terms: In medicine, off-label uses of medications can be productive when done with careful consideration of the risks and benefits. In the same way, sometimes, it may be possible to use SEL assessment for a purpose that is different from the main purposes for which it was designed and validated. Any off-label use of a medicine requires extra consideration of the likely benefit and the potential harms before proceeding. So too with assessment: If you are considering an off-label use, before charging forward, you (the user) have a responsibility to be very clear about the potential benefits and unintended consequences of doing so, and as much as possible to incorporate into your assessment process steps to maximize benefit and mitigate risk.

My hope is that you will use the process described here, along with worksheets in Table 3.1a and Table 3.1b, to identify and evaluate assessment candidates. If you do this, and you find the right tool for the job, you will be set up to collect high-impact SEL assessment data.

TABLE 3.2 Assessment Selection Worksheet

In our district, we will assess: _____

With the goal of:
- ❏ Understanding student strengths and needs to guide instruction and program investment
- ❏ Assessing student growth in response to our programs and practices
- ❏ Continuous improvement
- ❏ Progress monitoring

SKILL	SOCIAL AND EMOTIONAL DOMAIN	TYPE OF ASSESSMENT	CANDIDATE ASSESS-MENT	STRENGTHS	LIMITATIONS
1: _____ _____ _____ _____	❏ Comprehension ❏ Execution ❏ Self-control	❏ Direct assessment ❏ Teacher report ❏ Direct behavior rating ❏ Self-report ❏ Other:_____			
2: _____ _____ _____ _____	❏ Comprehension ❏ Execution ❏ Self-control	❏ Direct assessment ❏ Teacher report ❏ Direct behavior rating ❏ Self-report ❏ Other:_____			
3: _____ _____ _____ _____	❏ Comprehension ❏ Execution ❏ Self-control	❏ Direct assessment ❏ Teacher report ❏ Direct behavior rating ❏ Self-report ❏ Other:_____			
4: _____ _____ _____ _____	❏ Comprehension ❏ Execution ❏ Self-control	❏ Direct assessment ❏ Teacher report ❏ Direct behavior rating ❏ Self-report ❏ Other:_____			
5: _____ _____ _____ _____	❏ Comprehension ❏ Execution ❏ Self-control	❏ Direct assessment ❏ Teacher report ❏ Direct behavior rating ❏ Self-report ❏ Other:_____			

 Available to download at www.wwnorton.com/rd/mckown

Engaging Parents
as Partners

U p to now, this book has focused on the professional community of educators. All the steps described previously—defining SEL, clarifying
goals, and selecting an assessment—have focused on conversations between
educators and decisions and considerations made by educators. There is a
reason for this focus, of course—educators can and should play a key role in
supporting the development of the whole child, including social and emotional learning. But, as is the case with academic learning, parents are key
partners in this work. If the partnership is strong, it can amplify the impact
of educators' efforts. If the partnership is weak, educators will face a head-
wind in their work with students. This chapter is about the challenges and
opportunities in forging a strong working relationship between home and
school, with a focus on parent concerns that are likely to arise in response
to a social and emotional assessment initiative.

There are natural points of intersection that can serve as a foundation for building a strong home-school partnership. Most people, for example, agree that the abilities to interact successfully with others and to make and maintain positive relationships—also known as SEL—are valuable. Most people also agree that parents and educators can and should play an important role in supporting children's social and emotional development. In fact, research consistently finds that, whether they intend to or not, through their expectations, instructional practices, and relationships with students, teachers influence a host of social and emotional outcomes (Hamre & Pianta, 2001, Weinstein, 2002). Similarly, and not surprisingly, parenting styles—through parent levels of warmth, demandingness, and supportiveness—affect children's social and emotional development (Baumrind, 1971).

Having said all this, it is important to take active steps to engage parents as partners, particularly when it comes time to assess student social and emotional learning. A strong home-school connection can help reinforce the community's shared efforts to support student social and emotional growth. A weak connection can undermine those efforts.

Parent Discomfort

There are important benefits of engaging parents early and often in the process of SEL assessment. Perhaps the most immediate is that parents are sometimes anxious about or hostile to SEL assessment, and many of those negative feelings can be alleviated by clear and frequent communication. Parent discomfort with SEL, particularly SEL assessment, largely arises from five sources. First, some parents believe that social and emotional learning is a family matter and should therefore not be taught in schools. This is a case of home and school values coming into conflict. Second, parents might be concerned that the SEL assessment will cover highly sensitive topics such as sexuality, suicidal thoughts, drug use, and any number of other topics. Third, some parents are concerned that SEL assessment will lead to a diagnosis and the label, stigma and suboptimal educational placement that can come from it. Fourth, some parents are concerned that SEL assessment will show up on a report card and have a negative impact on future opportunity. The issue here is that parents do not want their students' school performance and academic record to include judgments about their social and emotional skills. Fifth, some parents may be concerned about cultural bias in assessment. This is an issue of trust in which parents have concerns that educators may not engage in SEL assessment in ways that benefit all students. We will discuss addressing the first four parent concerns next, and then spend some focused time exploring parent concerns about cultural bias.

Addressing Parent Concerns

The concerns described above are understandable. Even parents who support SEL programs and assessment might be concerned about these and other unintended consequences. The good news is that these concerns are as addressable as they are understandable. Several steps will prevent a lot of parent concerns and will help to address the concerns that remain.

First, you've already put in a lot of work to decide what you mean by social and emotional learning and what your goals are in assessing it. Along with communicating what SEL is and why you will assess it to colleagues in your district, communicate these issues to the parent community early and often, and obtain and use their input along the way where it is feasible. If parents have participated in this process, or at least have been regularly informed as it has evolved, you will have opportunities to engage with them over concerns and to enlist their support. Furthermore, the clearer you are about what SEL is and why you are going to assess it, and the more everyone in the district shares a clear understanding of these matters, the more easily anyone—classroom teacher, principal, social worker, assistant superintendent, school board member—will be able to confidently and competently field parent questions and concerns.

As we have discussed, the term "social and emotional learning" means different things to different people. The definitional uncertainty leaves room for worried parents to imagine that their child's school will be intrusively assessing sensitive personal matters. If you have defined what you mean and described your assessment goals, that groundwork will go a long way toward allaying parent concerns. Nevertheless, parents may still wonder what your assessment will ask of their child, what it will look like, what kinds of questions it will contain, and how exactly it is designed to assess what you have defined as social and emotional learning. In my work with parents, I have been repeatedly impressed by the calming effect a clear description of an assessment has on a concerned parent. For parents who worry that an SEL assessment will pry into all manner of intrusive matters, there is immediate relief, for example, in learning that for the SEL assessment, children will look at pictures and say what people are feeling, listen to illustrated stories and answer questions about the stories, and complete game-like tasks that involve sending rocket ships into space and making quick decisions about pairs of shapes. These are in fact quite innocuous tasks that measure skills that most people can understand and get behind. Describing the assessments clearly often reassures worried parents.

Many parents also want to know how you will use the assessment data, and transparency will help. Parents will likely wonder who will have access to assessment scores, whether those scores will be part of the child's cumulative record, and what kinds of decisions will be made on the basis of SEL assessment data. Note that parents become most concerned with the prospect that SEL assessments will be used to label or diagnose a child, will be part of their report card and permanent record, and will be shared inappropriately. Most parents support the use of SEL assessment to understand student strengths and needs so that educators can tailor instruction to build on student strengths and address student needs. If it is true, state explicitly that the assessment results will not result in a diagnosis or label, will not be on the report card, will not be part of the child's record, and will not influence educational placement. On the other hand, if the scores will end up in the student's record or will influence placement decisions, it will be important to be clear about this from the outset and be ready to offer a strong rationale for doing so, as well as evidence that the assessment you will be administering is valid for making these decisions.

Even if you do all of the above, some parents—generally, a very small minority—will object to SEL assessment. There are at least two ways to proceed. First, you can consider allowing parents to opt their children out of SEL assessment. This gives parents a meaningful choice in the matter, and will not likely greatly affect the assessment participation rate. However, there is a reasonable alternative. As a colleague who is a superintendent pointed out, schools routinely approve assessment plans with their board, and, in general, those plans do not include allowances for parents to opt their children out, because those assessments are necessary for educators to do their jobs effectively. If SEL assessment is as central to the effectiveness of the school as achievement tests, then it seems reasonable to treat them like any other assessment and not offer an opt-out option.

Cultural Bias

Parent concern that SEL assessment will be culturally biased is very serious and merits further exploration. In the last chapter, we discussed the issue of bias in terms of measurement equivalence, which concerns the technical properties of assessments. Sometimes, parents raise important questions about cultural appropriateness that move beyond technical considerations. Often originating from historical and ongoing inequity and unfairness are questions about whether educators will focus on the right things and use assessment data to support success for students from all backgrounds. The issues can be varied and a full exploration of them is beyond the scope of this book. Still, as this is often an important and challenging issue in SEL assessment, all who undertake SEL assessment would do well to think it through. To that end, I offer a brief description of four interrelated concerns about cultural appropriateness and some thoughts about addressing them.

First, some parents may question the cultural frame of reference for determining what SEL skill is, how it is enacted, and how it should be measured. They may point to a mismatch between the local community's culture and the apparent cultural backgrounds of people depicted in the assessment content, the description of the behaviors being assessed, or the situations in hypothetical vignettes. To some degree, this concern can be addressed with evidence of measurement equivalence. As I've argued earlier, the surface appearance of an assessment is not the best way to judge whether it works as well for one group as it does for another, and measurement equivalence can be evaluated quite rigorously.

However, evidence of measurement equivalence does not fully answer questions about cultural frame of reference. This is because the concern is not only about what *is* in the assessment; it's also about what is *not* in the assessment. Community members might raise concern that some important social-emotional skills that are critical in their community are not measured by the assessment in question. For example, for many children of color, the skill of code-switching, or being able to fluently and quickly cross between cultural contexts with different implicit rules of behavior, is a key skill for navigating the world, but is not often the target of assessment.

So do the SEL skills we have been discussing neglect important skills that are particular to some communities? Perhaps. However, there is a lot of evidence that the SEL skills we have been discussing do matter for all children regardless of their cultural background. For example, the most comprehensive meta-analysis, or quantitative summary, of SEL programs (Durlak, Weissberg, Dymnicki, Taylor, & Schellinger, 2011) found that SEL programs, when implemented well, lead to improved student outcomes. They looked for, but did not find, any evidence that the benefit of these programs was different for children from different ethnic or socioeconomic groups. This gives me confidence that the SEL skills that are the focus of our attention are important for all children and that assessing and addressing those skills will benefit all children. Nevertheless, other SEL skills may be important and the question of what is and what isn't assessed should be part of the early task of defining, with input from the community, what SEL skills are most important to assess and address (as described in Chapter 1). If you've been inclusive early on, this will likely not be a major concern.

Third, parents are sometimes concerned that educators will use SEL assessment data to describe inequalities as originating from individual students while discounting the broader context in which those inequalities come to be. For example, imagine a district with differential rates of disciplinary referrals for students from different ethnic groups. In this district, community members might be concerned that school leaders will use SEL assessment data to explain the discipline gap as arising from student SEL skill deficits and will discount the possibility that systemic biases and adult practices contribute to the disparity. Whether you are in a district with gaps like this or not, it will be wise to think carefully through how will you ensure—to your own satisfaction and to the satisfaction of the community you serve—that you will not become overly focused on student SEL skill to explain problems that require a focus on adult practices and school policies.

Fourth, parents are sometimes concerned that SEL assessment data will be used in ways that stigmatize their children. Looming large is the concern that by measuring student SEL skill, educators may be creating yet another way to document new kinds of racial or gender gaps and associated deficits. In addition to causing emotional pain, information about mean performance differences on SEL assessments between members of different groups can cause problems by, for example, subtly shaping what teachers expect from and how they treat their students. Furthermore, the benefit of this information is usually minimal. If your district is ethnically diverse, it will be important to develop and communicate plans to use SEL assessment data in ways that safeguard against the possibility that it will fruitlessly document deficits, with the risk of stigma and its consequences.

Like any major initiative in a multicultural society with a mixed record on race relations, SEL assessment has the potential to make things better, or to repeat the sins of the past. This places a special onus on all involved to proceed in ways that make thing better, while minimizing unintended negative consequences. Careful consideration of how to ensure cultural fairness runs through all stages of the process, including defining what SEL is, clarifying your assessment goals, selecting an assessment tool, and interpreting and using the assessment data. If these steps are engaged carefully and well, with regular communication between you and the community, you will be setting yourself up for high-impact SEL assessment that benefits teaching and learning for all students.

Beyond Assuaging Fear

So far, this chapter has been largely focused on how to connect with parents to preempt or address common concerns about social and emotional assessment. These are important steps to building trust, which is foundational to a good partnership. On the other hand, trust is not the entirety of the partnership. A strong partnership, with trust as its foundation, is about parents and educators working together towards the common goal of supporting student academic, social, and emotional learning. Once trust is established, a strong partnership can help ensure that parents and educators reinforce and support one another in their efforts to build on student social and emotional strengths and address student social and emotional needs.

The varied ways educators can enlist the support of parents are many and are beyond the scope of this book to discuss in detail. Whatever strategies a district uses to enlist the support of parents in academic learning may also be used to support social and emotional learning. At a minimum, parents will benefit from understanding what SEL assessment data say about students' social and emotional strengths and needs, the things teachers and others in the schools are doing to build on student strengths and address student needs, and the things they can do at home to support those efforts. If a district is using an evidence-based social and emotional learning program, this will provide regular and natural opportunities to share what students are learning and how those lessons can be reinforced at home.

Using the Data

Congratulations. You've done a lot of hard work. You got to clarity about what you mean when you say SEL. You've worked to articulate precise assessment goals. You've evaluated a range of assessment options to measure what you care about and achieve your assessment goals. You've selected the assessment for the job. All along, you've engaged parents as partners. And finally, in early October, you assessed every child in your district. The results are scored and reports summarizing findings are in hand. This is where things get exciting. Now that you have your student SEL assessment score reports, your most important task is to answer two questions.

The first is, "So what?" What do the assessment data reports say about the students who were assessed? Unfortunately, assessment scores won't interpret themselves. And so the team needs to spend time engaged together to review and interpret scores. This chapter will describe data use practices that will help answer the "So what?" question so that scores lead to insights. These data use practices are designed to increase the chances that SEL assessment data will have an impact on staff's understanding of their students.

Spending time sorting out what the assessment data say and what they mean will set you up to answer the second question: "Now what?" What positive actions can be taken based on the lessons learned from the assessment data? In addition to not interpreting themselves, data won't tell you what to do. This chapter will also help answer the crucial question, "Now what?" to convert insight into positive action, and to use cycles of data collection, interpretation, and planning as part of your work to continue getting better at supporting student social and emotional development.

The Data Won't Do Anything Unless You Use Them

You don't have to love data—scratch that: you don't even have to like data—to know that data will do absolutely nothing unless they are used. And not all actions count as using data. In fact, I have a very specific definition of "use" in mind. Using data means that defined groups, typically district administrators, principals, and teachers, engage in the following activities:

1. The team is created and prepares for assessment data review.
   - Identify a data review team member qualified to interpret assessment data.
   - Decide who else will be on the data review team.
   - Decide what level of assessment data will be reported.
   - Understand what assessment scores mean.

2. Individuals review the assessment reports to develop an initial interpretation of the data.

3. The team convenes to discuss the assessment scores. There are three meeting goals:
   - First, refine initial interpretations into an understanding of student strengths and needs.
   - Second, identify actions to build on student strengths and address student needs.
   - Third, commit to an action plan.

4. After reviewing the data and committing to a plan, implement the plan.

5. Repeat steps 2 through 4.

This model is designed to support data use that leads to insight and positive action, and reduce the risk of negative unintended consequences.

Let's consider a few actions that might seem like data use but that aren't. Emailing a summary of findings to the team is not data use. Including a discussion of findings in a staff meeting is part of use but not the whole thing. Talking about the SEL assessment findings in the lunchroom is great, but it is not really data use. District leadership interpreting the findings and sending a directive about what to do to building-level staff is not data use.

So how do you accomplish data use in the way we're talking about it? The mechanics of data use are going to differ from district to district and school to school, because each district and school will have different routines and practices already in place. In addition, each district will be at different stages of readiness to engage in the elements of data use described above. Because of this, there is no one-size-fits-all prescription for how to implement good data use practices.

Still, our working definition of data use provides a road map for districts to engage in high-impact and effective data use. To start, it can serve as the basis for an honest self-assessment of your district's readiness for effective data use. Table 5.1 is a self-assessment worksheet that can be used to decide which pieces are in place and which need work before your district is ready to use SEL assessment data to good effect. You may wish to conduct this needs assessment soon after the district has committed to undertaking SEL assessment. Use the worksheet in Table 5.1 for evaluating progress toward readiness, to plan for data use, and to evaluate how things went.

Let's walk through each of these, because simple though they may seem, they can be trickier than they look at first blush.

TABLE 5.1 Data Use Needs Assessment Worksheet

STEP		DATA USE REQUIREMENT	ARE WE READY?	WHAT ARE OUR CURRENT RESOURCES AND PRACTICES?	WHAT OTHER RESOURCES DO WE NEED TO SUCCEED?
1	Preparation	We have identified a team member who is expert on data use and interpretation.			
		We have selected members of the data review team.			
		We have decided on level of score reporting.			
		We understand what SEL assessment scores mean.			
2	Review, Reflect, Interpret, Plan	We have enough time to review data individually.			
		We have opportunities to discuss data.			
		How we discuss data helps us understand student strengths and needs.			
		We have opportunities to identify what to do based on what we learn.			
		We will commit to an action plan.			
3	Act	We have what is needed to implement our action plan.			

Identify Your Expert in Data Use

As was the case when selecting the right tool for the job, for most districts it will be important that someone on the data use team be a highly qualified user of assessment data. This could be a school psychologist or other educational professional with expertise in assessment and its interpretation. Whoever it is, they should have appropriate training and qualifications for interpreting and using assessment data of the kind you have collected for your intended purposes.

There is an important reason to include this person on the data use team, and they have a specific job to do. You see, assessment data are often quite evocative and—story-telling creatures that we are—we are likely to make all kinds of inferences from any assessment data. That is natural. However, some of the inferences we make and the stories we tell from data are not warranted because the assessment is not valid for making those inferences. For example, diagnosing a child as having an emotional disorder based on performance on the kinds of SEL assessments we are discussing would be a conclusion for which those assessments are generally not valid. Stories based on inferences that are not justified by the assessment data quickly become fiction. The team member who is a highly qualified assessment user can help ensure that interpretations and decisions based on the data are justified by the technical merits of the assessment and the data that come from it.

Decide Who is On the Data Review Team

Apart from the data use expert, choosing the team members will depend on your assessment goals and who will need to take action based on assessment results. A general principle for selecting data review team members is to identify people whose practice will benefit from or will be affected by SEL assessment data results. This will vary from setting to setting, which is why I'm leaving the team composition intentionally very broad. The important thing is to identify who is on the team and clarify what team membership will involve, described next.

Decide on Level of Score Reporting

An important consideration when using SEL assessment data concerns the level of aggregation of the scores. In fact, this matter should be settled well before data are collected and it is closely tied with your assessment goals. The most obvious (but paradoxically, often least useful and riskiest) level of data review is individual student score reports. For this level of reporting, the data team reviews the scores each child achieved on the SEL assessment. As we discussed in reviewing psychometrics, most SEL assessments are not valid for rendering diagnoses, labelling a child, or for making placement or other high-stakes decisions for individual students. If you identify an assessment validated for these purposes, in addition to meeting a high psychometric standard, users must be qualified to make those kinds of decisions. In general, if you are considering using SEL assessment data for diagnosis, placement, or other high-stakes decisions, proceed with caution.

Having said that, individual SEL assessment scores that meet technical quality standards may be useful formatively to decide how to focus instruction and support student learning. What does this look like? The team reviews individual student SEL assessment scores with the aim of identifying each student's social and emotional strengths and needs, much in the way teachers routinely use reading and math assessment data. Insights from individual assessment data review are used to differentiate instruction so that the teacher can work in a more individualized way to build on social and emotional strengths and to address social and emotional needs.

When interpreting SEL assessment data from individual student scores, it is important to be mindful of potential unintended consequences. Imagine, for example, that a student scores low on an SEL assessment. Imagine further that scores from this assessment are not very reliable, and in fact, the student's low score significantly underestimates her true abilities. It is possible in that situation that the assessment data would negatively affect how the teacher views and treats the student. To guard against this risk when using individual student data for formative purposes, think of a score as a source of hypotheses, not an immutable fact, and search for corroborating evidence about the child before coming to conclusions.

For many assessment goals, particularly those that focus on using assessment to improve teaching and learning, other levels of reporting may be more useful and less risky than using individual student scores. For example, aggregating student data at the classroom level can provide specific and clear information about the strengths and needs of that group of students—information that the teacher can use to adjust her instruction in ways that build on student strengths and address student needs, without risking the negative consequences that can arise from reviewing individual student scores. One benefit of this approach is that reliabilities in the .70 range are generally sufficient to safely and accurately interpret SEL assessment data aggregated at the classroom level or higher. The more I do this work, the more convinced I am that SEL assessment data presented clearly at the classroom level (and above) can be maximally beneficial for meeting most assessment goals while substantially reducing the risk of negative unintended consequences.

Understanding Scores

When you and your team receive the results of your SEL assessment, at whatever level meets your needs, will you know what to make of the scores? If everyone who is on the data use team understands what scores correspond to what skills, how the scores are scaled, and what score range reflects high, average, and low scores, you can answer "yes" to the question "Are we ready?"

Scores and Skills

The first component of understanding assessment scores is to know what skill each score in the assessment report reflects. Mastering this part of score consumption is key to understanding what the assessment scores tell you about student skills. In academic domains, this may be obvious—a test of long division skill has a clear meaning to a math teacher. In the social and emotional arena, as we have discussed, what the skills are can be less familiar. Not infrequently in my work with education partners, consumers of SEL assessment scores stop the conversation midstream and say, in effect, "Wait. What skill does this score reflect?"

Imagine, for example, a score report that includes, among other things, a score for cooperativeness. Each consumer of the score should know which score on the report corresponds to this skill. Furthermore, consumers should know what this skill looks like in practice. In one sense, this means that the consumer should have a passing familiarity with the items and assessment format used to measure cooperativeness (teacher ratings of the frequency of "Works well in groups," for example). In another sense, this means understanding how the skill would express itself in everyday peer interactions (student offers and receives help in group activities, for example). The important thing is to understand what skills are reflected in the scores and how they look in everyday life.

What's in a Number?

The next component of readiness to understand assessment scores is understanding the meaning of the numeric values that are in the score report. Some scores are mostly straightforward to understand. The meaning of the percentage of time a student was cooperative during an observation period is self-evident. What may be more difficult to know with scores like this is, what is a good score? Against what standard will you judge the meaning of this kind of score? If you use a predetermined standard, like 80%, that is criterion-referenced scoring. If you use the average and variability of the students in your district as the benchmark against which to judge individual student performance, that is norm-referenced scoring. For example, imagine that the average rate of cooperative behavior is 70%. With this frame of reference, 80% is above average.

Other assessments are nationally normed, with individual student performance on the assessment compared to a large sample of same-aged peers. For this kind of norm-referenced test, often a raw score, such as the number of items correct, or the average teacher rating, may be presented, along with some form of standard score. What is important in interpreting standard scores is knowing how the score is scaled. Some assessments will use what are called T scores, which have a mean of 50 and a standard deviation of 10. Others will use a standard score with a mean of 100 and a standard deviation of 15. Other scales are used as well.

Regardless, when you know the scale of the score—particularly, its mean and standard deviation—the score is interpretable as the distance of a child's performance from the average performance or same-aged peers in the assessed domain. Where T scores are presented, for example, a child who achieves a 50 is average for his or her age. For children whose score is not 50, the standard deviation can be used to judge how far above or below the mean a child's score is. Because T scores by definition have a standard deviation of 10, a child who achieves a score of 60 performed one standard deviation above the mean. A classroom of students whose average T score is 45 performs a half a standard deviation lower than average for peers from the standardization sample.

Generally, one standard deviation above or below the mean is a significant distance from average. If scores are normally distributed, and you can generally assume this, a student who scores one standard deviation above the mean has scored better than 84% of her peers. A student who scores one standard deviation below the mean has scored better than 16% of his peers. Plus or minus one standard deviation is commonly used refer to the average range. However, there is no hard and fast rule to determine the boundary between good enough and not good enough performance. Often, assessment developers will characterize performance levels (for example, low, average, high, very high). If they do not, you may impose cut points on the scores to define performance levels but realize that any cutoff is, at least in part, arbitrary.

In addition to understanding how the scores from a norm-referenced assessment are scaled, review the characteristics of the sample on which the assessment was normed, so you can judge the extent to which the norming sample is similar to or different from your students.

Once you understand the skill that each score reflects, and you understand the meaning of the numbers, you have fulfilled the first data use requirement. If you and your team do not feel comfortable either with your grasp of the skill each score reflects or the meaning of the numbers, three resources may be helpful. The first is the assessment manual. It should provide clarity around these two issues. If, after reviewing the manual, you still feel some mental murk, contact the test publisher and talk to an actual person until you are satisfied you understand, or engage them to provide professional development to you and your staff. Finally, the member of your data review team with expertise in interpreting test scores can be invaluable here—armed with an understanding of the arcana of test scoring and interpretation, he or she can quickly help the rest of the team master this part of data use for any assessment. They can train you and your team to a high level of comfort and proficiency.

Routines for Review, Reflection, Interpretation, and Planning

Even if you understand what skills each score reflects, and you understand what the numbers mean, that won't get you very far unless everyone on the team has a chance to review the score reports. The heart of the data review process will happen in team discussions, described in more detail next. But there is an important step to complete before the team convenes.

Opportunities to Review Data

Specifically, the very first step is for each member of the team to take time to review the assessment reports independently. This means spending enough undistracted time with the data to develop an initial interpretation of what the data say about student strengths and needs. No more. No less. It doesn't mean hastily reviewing an emailed summary of the findings three minutes before the team meeting. After the initial review of data, each person should be able to answer the question, "What is your understanding of our students' social-emotional strengths and social-emotional needs, and what questions does this raise for you?"

Opportunities to Discuss Data

Individual data review primes the pump for productive team data review. The purpose of the team meeting is to bring together those who will use SEL assessment data to come to greater clarity. First, let me say that I will not make specific recommendations about who should be at the meeting, how frequently meetings should convene, how long they should last, and other important considerations. What I will say is that in the best of all worlds, team discussions about SEL assessment data will be integrated into ongoing routines in a way that maximizes the chance that the meetings will happen and that their learning objectives will be fulfilled. Some school districts, for example, convene regular grade-level team meetings to review test data. In those schools, adding social-emotional assessment data to reading and math test scores is relatively straightforward. Other districts may need to establish data review teams and procedures from scratch. Even in those cases, it is best to try to commandeer some time from standing meetings rather than create yet another meeting to attend.

Now that you've set the stage, you are ready to answer two critical questions we described previously: "So what?" and "Now what?"

So What?

Answering the question, "So what?" involves convening the team to get clear about the facts, and interpreting their meaning in preparation for planning positive action. Whatever the forum and format, answering the question, "So what?" involves three tasks (Coburn & Turner, 2011):

1. Come to a common understanding of what the assessment data say.
2. Interpret what the assessment data mean.
3. Generate testable hypotheses about student social-emotional skill development.

This is a variant of an instructional approach an educator friend called "see, think, wonder." The first step is to describe what is seen. Coming to an understanding of what the assessment data say is about first noticing the facts that the data represent without judgment. This means looking at all the data for all the students, not picking out a single fact that supports a preconception about student social and emotional learning. This is not easy to do, as it is deeply ingrained in human nature to quickly seek facts that confirm our ideas of the world and to impose a narrative on the data that implies judgment.

Stage 1: See

In this stage—the "see" portion of see, think, wonder—the conversation focuses strictly on the question, what are the facts? The facilitator should set clear ground rules. Let's call the rules of the see phase "Jack Webb rules" (after the hard-boiled detective whose recurrent line was, "Just the facts, ma'am"). The facilitator should enforce Jack Webb rules, looking out for any straying into interpretation. So, for example, it is fair game to say, "I see that in these two areas A and B, 45% of students meet the standard; in these three areas X, Y, and Z, 15% of students meet the standard." These assertions are a description of facts represented in the assessment data. It is straying into interpretation to say, "Our students show strengths in A and B and weaknesses in X, Y, and Z." Describing the data in terms of strengths and weaknesses goes beyond the surface facts and begins to apply an interpretive judgment to the data. There is nothing wrong with that kind of judgment, but before interpretation, it is important to review and summarize the facts presented by the data. The facilitator's job is to keep the team reporting facts, with the prompt being, "What else do you notice?," or something like it, until the team has come to a complete description of the major facts presented by the data report. There's no right answer dictating when you've reached this stage. But don't mistake silence for being done—you want to make sure most everyone has contributed, and when their observations start to overlap, this is a sign that you are nearing the end of this phase of the discussion.

Stage 2: Think

In the next stage, the "think" stage of the see, think, wonder cycle, participants can start making meaning of the data by imposing interpretations of the data onto the facts. The question participants are answering in this phase is, what do these facts make you think? The facilitator can now permit participants to start forming interpretations of the meaning of the facts they just finished reviewing. Here are some fair interpretations:

- "I think the high scores on cooperative behavior show that our students are generally kind to one another, but there are a few outliers."
- "The low scores on social problem solving show that we have room to work on that skill, even though some of our students are clearly really good at this."
- "It doesn't surprise me that our students are low on ratings of problem behavior. I am a bit surprised though that they were below average on socially skilled behavior."

In all these examples, the respondents have moved past the facts to their interpretation of the facts. Note, however, that the interpretations are all clearly referring to a fact. They are interpretations that are based upon and supported by the facts.

There are a couple of things for the facilitator to look out for here. First are interpretive statements that are not clearly tied to and supported by the facts. This can come in the form of an overly general statement such as,

"There aren't any surprises here," or, "Looks like we have a lot of work to do." Follow-up questions asking for specifics can help keep the conversation grounded. Examples include, "What exactly did you see that wasn't a surprise? Were there any things that did not fit your expectations?" And, "When you say we have a lot of work to do here, what is it in the data that makes you say that? What do you think it means we have to work on?"

A second issue to keep in check is action steps or hypotheses disguised as think statements. For example, someone might say, "I think we need to use our problem-solving skills curriculum to address weakness in this area." Yes, this sentence does start with "I think," but it is really a call to a specific action. Actions are good, and will be an essential part of the conversation, but for this phase, remember that the goal is to interpret the meaning of the scores, not to start formulating actions.

A third issue to keep in check is the introduction of debate. Debate and disagreement can be productive, but it can inhibit the creative brainstorming that should be at the heart of this conversation. So if someone says, "I see what you're saying, but . . ." or "I see it differently," or, more plainly, "I disagree," the facilitator's job is to encourage each individual to state their thoughts, not in relation to or in disagreement with others' thoughts. The general principle here is that all reasonable interpretations are fair game in making sense of the data, even if the interpretations don't fit together or perfectly agree.

As was the case during the see phase of the conversation, the facilitator's job is to solicit thoughts from participants until the group has articulated multiple interpretations of the data. As was the case with the see part of the discussion, there's no right answer to indicate that this part of the discussion has run its course. The facilitator's job is to elicit interpretations until the well has started to run dry. Again, don't mistake silence for being done, because that may reflect reluctance or reticence rather than a completed conversation.

Stage 3: Wonder

The final phase of this conversation is the wonder part of "see, think, wonder," and it involves generating testable hypotheses, some of which may form the basis for action steps. In this phase of the conversation, discussion participants are encouraged to ask questions that the data raised, often about what might be giving rise to the pattern of data, and how the assessment data might be related to other areas of functioning. Respondents are encouraged to start their responses with, "I wonder . . ." Examples might be, "I wonder if the lower scores on empathy are associated with increases in video game usage," or "I wonder if our kids are missing out on opportunities to learn social problem solving because the adults intervene to solve problems and kids don't learn to work them out," or "I wonder whether the troubles we're seeing on measures of self-control are contributing to my difficulties with classroom management." Note that these examples focus on areas of concern, which they often will. In this part of the conversation, the facilitator should encourage wondering about bright spots that will undoubtedly be evident in the data. In addition to making sense of challenges, this can be a forum for celebrating successes.

All these statements above draw connections between what the respondents have described in the see phase and interpreted in the think phase and other matters that are important to them. Each of these statements can be easily rephrased as a testable hypothesis—the more children play video games, the more difficulty they will have empathizing with others. The more adults solve children's problems for them, the less children will learn effective social problem-solving skills. And so on. I'm not making any claims about the accuracy of the hypotheses. But you can see how wondering about the data can easily generate interesting and testable hypotheses, some of which may be grounds for action.

It is the facilitator's job in this part of the discussion to elicit as many wonder statements as possible. The facilitator should be mindful of whether the wondering is focused on matters in the teachers' sphere of influence. For example, "I wonder whether the low scores on self-control reflect the constant presence of technology" focuses on something the teachers don't have much say over. "I wonder whether the low scores on self-control are related to some of the behavioral challenges I'm seeing in my class," on the other hand, brings the discussion into the sphere of the teacher's influence. Encourage the team to wonder about the connection between the SEL scores and what happens in class. As in the other phases, prevent debate and focus on generating ideas. The only corrective feedback required is if the participants begin to offer statements that are not wonder statements. Then, gently redirect the conversation back to that purpose.

Now What?

See, think, wonder sets the group up to discuss what they might do in response to what they see in the data, what they think about its meaning, and their hypotheses about patterns in the data. If the see, think, wonder part of the conversation helped discussion participants answer the question "So what?," this part of the conversation is geared toward answering the question, "Now what?" And the facilitator's goal here is to clarify what specifically the team wants to accomplish and identify a manageable number of action steps that can be taken in a reasonable amount of time that are designed to achieve these goals.

You know already that I'm a big proponent of being clear about goals. Here is another place where goal clarity is at least half the battle. The SEL assessment data review process you have already undertaken should result in, or at least strongly inform, a clear set of skill development goals. Once you clarify what skills you want to nurture, this serves to focus the search for actions you can take to achieve your goals. So the task here is to identify what strengths are the building blocks of success and what needs are the focus of extra or new efforts. In short, your job is to identify skill development goals that include what skills are to be developed, by how much, and in what time frame.

Once a skill development goal is clear, there are at least two ways one can approach the question of "Now what?" The first place to look for productive action steps is in the proverbial mirror. Specifically, you'll look first for the everyday effective practices that are bright spots among your team. These are instructional approaches or activities that seem likely to be addressing the goal but are not implemented widely, systematically, or intensively. In addition, these are practices that, if everyone did them more frequently or intensively, would likely advance your goals. This is a good place to start because it is highly likely that among the collective wisdom, professional development, and hard-won experiences of the team, for every social-emotional instructional goal, someone on the team will have good ideas about what can be done to meet the goal.

Beware of a potential pitfall. If you hear members of the team saying something like, "Oh, we already do that," that is a red flag that signals the high likelihood that the speaker, and anyone who is convinced by that argument, will do nothing new. When that comes up, remind everyone that this is the time to stretch and find new or better ways to support student learning, not to continue unchanged. Assume the team is already doing good things to support student social and emotional development and encourage them to consider how they could do these things more frequently, intensively, and effectively. We are all in the learning business, after all, which means continually looking for new ways to understand and address the challenges before us.

There is a second kind of looking in the mirror. Specifically, in addition to existing collective professional wisdom, there may already be useful resources among the district's inventory of programs, interventions, personnel, and resources. There may be an opportunity, with a little effort and some creativity, to use those existing resources to address student social-emotional goals. Many schools who use our assessments, for example, have adopted one of the CASEL select evidence-based social and emotional curricula (Weissberg, Goren, Mitrovic, & Dusenbury, 2013). Each of those programs has a thoughtfully constructed scope and sequence of distinct lessons, activities, and materials focused on developing important social-emotional skills. It may be possible, then, to adapt the curriculum to address your high-priority skill development goals. Some curriculum providers will advise against violating the lesson sequence, as skills may build on one another. However, you may find that it will be helpful to emphasize some units or lessons more strongly than others, to preview lessons that reflect areas of need, and to begin to practice skills that need the most work early and often, using the principles and exercises included in the SEL curriculum.

Once you've taken an inventory of the resources available to you already—wisdom, program investments, curricula, and any other relevant resource, it's time to look outward. There are in fact many social and emotional learning programs available that support your priority skill development goals. Those resources come in several forms. First are the kinds of evidence-based SEL programs just described. Second are intensive teacher professional development experiences designed to help teachers develop the kinds of strong relationships and positive classroom environments that are conducive to social-emotional skill development. Third are supplementary materials—a growing number of interactive training technologies or "serious games," instructional videos, and other resources that may be deployed rather easily to address specific needs. As you review options, I urge you to consider the strength of the evidence that, when implemented well, the strategy will have a positive impact.

Program investments to build on social-emotional strengths and address social-emotional needs should and generally will be made after careful deliberation and integration with the district's strategic plan to meet educational priorities. It is beyond the scope of this book to discuss in depth the process for deciding what SEL resources are the right investments to meet a district's strategic priorities. If you're reading this book and you've taken the trouble to assess student social-emotional learning, it's likely you work in a district that already prioritizes student social-emotional development. The process described in this book—defining SEL, clarifying your assessment goals, selecting the right tool for the job, and engaging in a thoughtful deliberative process to interpret and make decisions based on the data—may serve as a model for reviewing existing resources and selecting external resources needed to achieve your goals for student academic, social, and emotional success.

Commitment and Action

After you've made sense of the data, clarified your skill development goals, and identified existing and new resources you need to achieve those goals, it's time to act. Rather, it's time to make a commitment to action, which involves stating the specific and measurable actions you will take to reach the student skill development goals. This should also involve a commitment to bringing the resources teachers need—professional development, peer mentoring, and program supports—to engage in new activities and cover new content to achieve student skill development goals. This commitment is a commitment of the entire community—teachers, administrators, and, if you've set things up well, the parent community. All there is to do at this point is put the plan into action, monitor its implementation, and, after you've given it some time to work, assess student SEL again to take stock of student progress.

Becoming a Learning Organization

Imagine you've done everything by the book. You engaged in an organized and vigorous process of defining SEL, clarifying your goals, selecting your assessments, and establishing and executing effective data use. Out of your data use meetings, you developed insights from the data and used those insights to identify specific skill development goals that build on your students' strengths and address their needs. You identified existing and new resources needed to achieve the skill development goals. Everyone committed to a specific action plan and then put the plan into action. After a reasonable interval implementing the plan, you reassessed student SEL skill.

Imagine that you found, on balance, that nothing had changed.

I say this not to be a downer—of course, I hope that through your vigorous and organized actions you move the needle and detect that movement very quickly. But sometimes life doesn't cooperate. Behavior change is hard for adults and for children, and that fact may make progress slower than you would like. So maybe implementation was not as intensive as it needed to be. Or maybe it was, and students are beginning to turn around, but things haven't been in place long enough to detect improvement. Or maybe your assessment is not measuring the things that are actually getting better.

Whatever the case, my message to you is this: If you've followed the program outlined in this book, you have begun a process that tilts the balance in favor of success. Using data to understand how things are going and what you will do is not a one-and-done endeavor. Plan to assess regularly. Plan to engage in vigorous data use practices after every assessment wave. Develop a realistic time frame for improvement in educational practice and student outcomes to set expectations that are ambitious but achievable. Plan to continue to identify student strengths and needs and use what you learn each time you do this to inform how you work with your students, using local and external resources. And plan to do this over and over and over again. Sustained improvement will happen with sustained effort, and a sustained commitment to using appropriate assessment data to inform decision making about how to support teacher success and student social and emotional development.

The Future of
SEL Assessment

Now is a dynamic time in the field of SEL assessment. Interest in children's social and emotional learning is growing seemingly by the day. Along with this, educators are increasingly asking what they can do to assess student social-emotional skills to help teachers understand their students and teach them as effectively as possible.

Taking Stock

Developers of SEL curricula and programs have been at this for several decades, resulting in resources that, if used well and with enough intensity, are likely to support student success. In contrast, with a couple of noteworthy exceptions, less attention and fewer resources have been devoted to developing and field testing the kinds of assessments educators need to achieve the varied assessment goals that will support teacher success and student social and emotional development.

This is changing. A growing number of companies have started to offer high-quality social and emotional assessment systems that are designed for applied use in educational settings. Many of these promising assessments are well-suited to meeting some of the SEL assessment needs of educators. But there is more work to be done before the field can lay claim to a portfolio of assessment offerings that are suited to the varied assessment needs of educators and that span K to 12. Surely this will require a substantial investment of time and money to fill out the portfolio of much-needed assessments. Whether this investment is forthcoming is an open question.

Important Developments

There are signs that things are changing. Several ongoing working groups are wrestling with important questions about how to build the field of social and emotional assessment in a way that has maximum impact and benefit for all students. The Funders' Collaborative for Innovative Measurement, for example, a coalition of foundations, supports an SEL assessment work group that is undertaking sustained work to: (1) reconcile disparate definitions of SEL; (2) create a repository of SEL assessments for researchers and practitioners; (3) create an assessment guide, primarily for practitioners; and (4) mount an annual design challenge to shine a light on and stimulate the development of innovative emerging SEL assessments. With funding from the Spencer Foundation, the Buros Center for Testing has brought together a group of experts to develop guidelines for SEL assessment use. Large test companies are beginning to offer social and emotional assessments. And educators are increasingly experimenting with SEL assessment for continuous improvements. The CORE districts in California, for example, use SEL assessment as part of their accountability framework and use what they learn about student SEL to support school improvement efforts.

Looking Forward

Predicting the future is a tricky business, but from where I sit, there are likely to be three developments in the arena of SEL assessment. Okay, I'll admit, this is somewhere between a prediction and a wish, because I believe these are the developments the field needs to have a robust and healthy marketplace of SEL assessments. First, creative assessment developers—hopefully in collaboration with educators—will continue to design and field innovative assessments designed to meet educators' needs. Second, assessment developers will form partnerships with curriculum and intervention providers so that educators who undertake assessments will have turnkey solutions to the problems they identify, and educators who use programs can use them in targeted, data-informed ways that magnify their benefit to students. Third, state and federal policy makers will craft policies that stimulate the increased and productive focus on SEL and its assessment. Those policies might, for example, set expectations for what SEL skills children should know and be able to demonstrate at different grade levels. They might incentivize the adoption of evidence-based SEL programs and rigorous assessments. They might require preservice teacher training on student social-emotional development. And they might support sustained investment in assessment research and development (McKown, 2017a).

How much of this comes to pass is anybody's guess. However things unfold, it seems likely that SEL assessment options will increase with time. As this happens, educators will have a larger range of options to consider to meet their social and emotional assessment needs. This is a good problem to have. As the number of options increases, it will remain important to recognize that the assessment itself is only one piece of a larger puzzle. Assessment of any kind, including SEL assessment, takes place in complex systems in which different constituents, including parents, have different concerns, goals and ideas, and in which assessment data can be interpreted and used differently by different people. Amid this complexity, it is wise to consider assessment as a process that involves defining what you want to assess, clarifying your goals for undertaking assessment, selecting assessment tools based on your definition and goals, and engaging in rigorous and ongoing data use and action cycles.

The specific assessment used is important, but just as important are the preparatory activities that precede assessment selection and administration and the discussion and decision-making processes that follow. My fervent hope is that any educator who wishes to assess student SEL puts in the time and effort to set themselves up for success and follows assessment with actions that measurably improve the success of teachers and the lives of their students.

References

Baumrind, D. (1971). Current patterns of parental authority. *Developmental Psychology, 4,* 1–103.

Beauchamp, M. H., & Anderson, V. (2010). SOCIAL: An integrative framework for the development of social skills. *Psychological Bulletin, 136,* 39–64. doi:10.1037/a0017768

Coburn, C.E., & Turner, E.O. (2011). Research on data use: A framework and analysis. *Measurement, 9,* 173–206

DiPerna, J. C., Volpe, R. J., & Elliott, S. N. (2002). A model of academic enablers and elementary reading/language arts achievement. *School Psychology Review, 31,* 298–312.

Duckworth, A. L., Gendler, T. S., & Gross, J. J. (2014). Self-control in school-age children. *Educational Psychologist, 49*(3), 199–217.

Duckworth, A.L., Peterson, C., Matthews, M.D., & Kelly, D.R. (2007). Grit: Perseverance and passion for long-term goals. *Journal of Personality and Social Psychology, 92*(6), 1087–1101.

Durlak, J.A., Weissberg, R.P., Dymnicki, A.B., Taylor, R.D., & Schellinger, K.B. (2011). The impact of enhancing students' social and emotional learning: A meta-analysis of school-based universal interventions. *Child Development, 82,* 405–432.

Durlak, J. A., Domitrovich, C. E., Weissberg, R. P., & Gullotta, T. P. (Eds.). *The handbook of social and emotional learning.* New York: Guilford.

Dusenbury, L., Dermody, C., & Weissberg, R. P. (2018). *2018 state scorecard scan: More states are supporting social and emotional learning.* Chicago: Collaborative for Academic Social and Emotional Learning.

Dweck, C. S. (2006). *Mindset: The New Psychology of Success.* New York: Ballantine.

Elias, M. J., & Ferrito, J. J. (2016). *The other side of the report card.* Thousand Oaks, CA: Corwin.

Gross, J. J. (1998). The emerging field of emotion regulation: An integrative review. *Review of General Psychology, 2,* 271–299.

Halberstadt, A. G., Denham, S. A., & Dunsmore, J. C. (2001). Affective social competence. *Social Development, 10,* 79–119. doi:10.1111/1467-9507.00150

Hamre, B. K., & Pianta, R. C. (2001). Early teacher-child relationships and the trajectory of children's school outcomes through eighth grade. *Child Development, 72,* 625–638.

Jones, S. M., & Bouffard, S. M. (2012). Social and emotional learning in schools: From programs to strategies. *SRCD Social Policy Report, 26,* 3–33.

Lemirese, E. A., & Arsinio, W. F. (2000). An integrated model of emotion processes and cognition in social information processing. *Child Development, 71,* 107–118.

Lipton, M. E., & Nowicki, S. (2009). The social-emotional learning framework (SELF): A guide for understanding brain-based social-emotional learning impairments. *Journal of Developmental Processes, 4,* 99–115.

McKown, C. (2017a). Social and emotional learning: A policy vision for the future. *Future of Children, 29,* 1–5.

McKown, C. (2017b). Social-emotional assessment, performance, and standards. *Future of Children, 29,* 157–178.

Moffitt, T. E., Arseneault, L., Belsky, D., Dickson, N., Hancox, R. J., Harrington, H., . . . Caspi, A. (2011). A gradient of childhood self-control predicts health, wealth, and public safety. *PNAS Proceedings of the National Academy of Sciences of the United States of America, 108,* 2693–2698. doi:10.1073/pnas.1010076108

Nagaoka, J., Farrington, C. A., Ehrlich, S. B., & Heath, R. D. (2015). *Foundations for young adult success: A developmental framework.* Chicago: University of Chicago Consortium on School Research.

National Research Council. (2012). *Education for life and work: Developing transferable knowledge and skills in the 21st century.* Washington, DC: National Academies Press.

Newcomb, A. F., Bukowski, W. M., & Pattee, L. (1993). Children's peer relations: A meta-analytic review of popular, rejected, neglected, controversial, and average sociometric status. *Psychological Bulletin, 113,* 99–128.

Obradovic, J. Sulik, M. J., Finch, J. E., & Tirado-Strayer, N. (2018). Assessing students' executive functions in the classroom: Validating a scalable group-based procedure. *Journal of Applied Developmental Psychology, 55,* 4–13.

Weinstein, R.S. (2002). *Reaching higher: The power of expectations in schooling.* Cambridge, MA: Harvard University Press.

Weissberg, R. P., Goren, P., Domitrovich, C., & Dusenbury, L. (2013). *Effective social and emotional learning programs: Preschool and elementary school edition.* Chicago: CASEL.

Whitcomb, S., & Merrell, K. W. (2012). *Behavioral, social, and emotional assessment of children and adolescents.* New York: Routledge.

Index

Note: Italicized page locators refer to figures; tables are noted with a *t*.

accountability
    high-stakes, SEL assessment and, 18
    low-stakes, SEL assessment and, 17
action, making commitment to, 70*t*, 89
administrators, commitment to action
        and, 89
aggregation
    of the scores, level of, 70*t*, 72–74
    of student data, at classroom level, 73–74
assessment
    complex systems and process of, 95
    direct, 30*t*, 31*t*, 33
    formative, xviii, 17, 20–21, 29, 31*t*, 52
    regular, planning for, 90
    strengths and weaknesses of, 52

summative, xviii, 17
    see also candidate assessment tools; SEL
        assessment
assessment data
    challenges related to, xxii–xxiii
    interpreting, 73–74
    see also data
assessment developers
    consulting with, 52–53
    partnerships with curriculum and
        intervention providers, 94
assessment reports, reviewing, 68
Assessment Selection worksheet, 54*t*
averages, of scores, 76, 77
aversive behavior, 10

behavioral assessment, challenges in, 49
behavioral dysregulation, rating scales
    and, 36
behavior change, 90
behavior(s)
    observable, 34
    positive, 9–10
    socially aversive, 10
    see also direct behavior ratings (DBRs)
bias
    cultural, parental concern with,
        60–64
    evaluating, 47–48
brainstorming, 83
Buros Center for Testing, 94

California, CORE districts in, 94
candidate assessment tools
    evaluating, 39–50
    identifying, resources for, 37–38
    "off-label" use of, 52, 53
    selecting, 50–51, 54*t*
    wrong tools for the job, 51–53
CASEL. *see* Collaborative for Academic
    Social and Emotional Learning
    (CASEL)
clarity of purpose, high-impact assessment
    and, xviii
code-switching, 61
Collaborative for Academic Social and
    Emotional Learning (CASEL), xix
    five major components of SEL, 5, 6
    online assessment guide, 37, 38

evidence-based social and emotional
    curricula, 87–88
comprehension skills, 12, 38
    Defining SEL worksheet category, 13*t*,
        14
    description of, 9
    methods suited to measurement of,
        32–33
confirmatory factor analysis, 48
continuous improvement, 17, 29, 31*t*
convergent validity, 44
correlation coefficients, 46
criterion-referenced scoring, 76
criterion-related validity, 44–45, 46
cultural appropriateness, concerns about
    cultural frame of reference and, 61
    neglect of important skills and, 61–62
    risk of stigma and, 63
    systemic bias and, 62–63
cultural bias in SEL assessment, parental
    concern with, 57, 60–64
cultural fairness, ensuring, 63–64
curriculum providers, assessment devel-
    oper partnerships and, 94

data review process
    answering "now what?" question in, 79,
        86–87
    answering "so what?" question in, 79,
        80
    developing hypotheses from, 86
    discussing data in, opportunities for,
        70*t*, 79

inferences made from, 71
  reviewing data in, opportunities for, 70t, 78–79
data review team, 68
  choosing members of, 70t, 72
  consulting with, 78
  goal clarity and, 86
  pitfalls to avoid with, 87
data use
  activities tied to, 67–68
  commitment and action step, 70t, 89
  high-impact and effective, 69
  mechanics of, 69
  preparation steps, 70t, 71–78
  review, reflect, interpret, plan steps, 70t, 78–89
  working definition of, 69
Data Use Needs Assessment worksheet, 70t
DBRs. *see* direct behavior ratings (DBRs)
debate, preventing, 83, 85
Defining SEL worksheet, 13t
diagnoses
  assessment data and, cautionary note, 72–73
  SEL assessment and, 18
direct assessment, 29
  assessing social and emotional comprehension with, 33
  description of, and assessment goal, 31t
  description of, strengths and limitations, 30t
  of self-control, 35

direct behavior ratings (DBRs), 29, 42
  description, strengths and limitations, 30t
  description and assessment goal, 31t
  observed behaviors assessed with, 34
discipline gap, 62, 63
discriminant validity, 44
district leadership, SEL definition approval and, 15

emotional dysregulation, 10
emotion regulation, 33
ethnic diversity and SEL assessments, 63
execution skills, 9–10, 12, 38
  Defining SEL worksheet category, 13t, 14
  description of, 9
  methods suited to measurement of, 34
executive functions, 35
expert in data use
  identifying, 70t, 71
  training and qualifications for, 71

face validity, 44
facial expressions, reading, 33
factor analysis, 45
formative assessment, xviii, 17, 20–21, 29, 31t, 52
Funders' Collaborative for Innovative Measurement, SEL assessment goals, 93

games, "serious," 88
goal clarity
  achieving, difficulties in, xviii–xix

goal clarity (*continued*)
  bottom-up or grassroots inspiration and, 23
  communicating to principals, teachers, and parent community, 26
  getting to, 22–26
  SEL assessment and, 18–19, 20, 21–22
  SEL assessment data review process and, 86
  summarizing findings and, 25–26
  top-down or executive inspiration and, 22–23
grit
  definition of, 36
  self-control and, 11
growth mind-set, 11

high-stakes decisions, assessment data and, cautionary note, 73
home-school partnership, strong, 55–56
hypotheses
  testable, about SEL skill development, 80
  testable, generating, 84, 85

impulsivity
  defining, 11
  measuring, 36
individual student data
  score reports, 72
  using for formative purposes, 73
innovative assessments, 94

inspiration
  bottom-up or grassroots, 23
  channeling, 23–24
  top-down or executive, 22–23
instructional videos, 88
interactive training technologies, 88
internal consistency reliability, 40–41, 42
interpersonal interactions, execution skills and, 9–10
inter-rater reliability, 41–43
intervention providers, assessment developer partnerships and, 94
item equivalence, 48
item response theory method, 48

learning organization, moving toward becoming, 90–91

math assessment data, 73
math test scores, SEL assessment data added to, 79
mean, standard deviation above or below, 77
mean deviation, in scores, 76
measurement equivalence, 39, 47–50, 60
  configural invariance, 48–49
  complexity of, 50
  cultural frame of reference and, 61
  flawed ways to evaluate possible bias in, 47–48
  types of, 48–49
memory
  short-term, 35
  working, 35

metric invariance, 49
mission statement, 12
multi-tiered systems of support (MTSS),
29, 31t

nonverbal cues, reading, 9
norming sample, 77
norm-referenced scoring, 76, 77
numeric values, understanding meaning
of, 75–78

observable behaviors, assessing, 34
observation, 28–29
description of, strengths and limitations, 30t
description of and assessment goal,
31t
open-ended questions, 24

parenting styles, children's social and
emotional development and, 56
parents
addressing concerns of, 57–60
building strong partnership with,
64–65
commitment to action and, 89
complexity surrounding assessment
and, 95
cultural bias concerns of, 60–64
discomfort with SEL, 56–57
engaging as partners, xxii, xxvi, 55–65
establishing trust with, 64
partnership with educators, 55–56

peer mentoring, commitment to action
and, 89
peer nomination, 29
barriers to use of, 36
description of, and assessment goal,
31t
description of, strengths and limitations, 30t
observed behaviors assessed with, 34
performance levels, characterizing, 77
perseverance, self-control and, 11
perspective-taking, 14
placement, assessment data and, cautionary note, 73
policy making, SEL assessment and, 94
problems, reframing, 10
professional development, commitment to
action and, 89
program evaluation, 17, 29, 31t
progress monitoring, 17, 52
psychometrics, consumer's guide to,
39–50
measurement equivalence, 39, 47–50
reliability, 39–43
validity, 39, 43–46
psychometrics, definition of, 39

questions, open-ended, 24

race, SEL assessments and, 63
RAND Corporation, social and emotional
assessments catalog, 37, 38
Rasch method, 48

rating scales, 28
  behavioral dysregulation measurement and, 36
  observed behaviors assessed with, 34
raw scores, 76
reading assessment data, 73
reading skills, social and emotional comprehension and, 33
reading test scores, SEL assessment data added to, 79
relationship skills, as core SEL competency, 5, 6
reliability, 39–43
  consistency across items, 40–41
  consistency across rates, 41–43
  consistency across time, 41
  reproducibility of scores and, 39
  validity vs., 43
reliability coefficients, 46
resources
  commitment to action and, 89
  high-quality assessment systems, 93
  local and external, 91
  taking inventory of, 88
responsible decision-making, as core SEL competency, 5, 6

scalar invariance, 49
scaling of scores, 76, 77
school districts
  data use and, 69
  grade-level team meetings and, 79

score reporting, deciding on level of, 70*t*, 72–74
score(s)
  leading to insights, 67
  normal distribution of, 77
  numeric values and, 75–78
  raw, 76
  reliability of, 39, 42
  reviewing and interpreting, 66–67
  scaling of, 76, 77
  skills and, 74–75, 77
  as source of hypotheses, 73
  understanding, 70*t*, 74–78
screening, SEL assessment and, 17
"see, think, wonder" approach, stages in, 80–85
  "see" (stage 1), 81
  "think" (stage 2), 82–84
  "wonder" (stage 3), 84–85
SEL assessment
  clear goals and, 18–19, 20, 21–22
  cultural bias concern of parents and, 60–64
  dynamic time for, 92
  evaluating technical properties of, 51
  inspiration and, 22–24
  methods of, 30*t*
  parental discomfort and, 56–57, 58–59
  parental objection to, 60
  risks associated with, 19–20
  team discussions about, 79

understanding varied goals related to, 24–25

undertaking, common reasons for, 17–18

see also data use; goal clarity

SEL assessment, future of, 92–95

important developments in, 93–94

increased options and, 95

innovative assessments, 94

partnerships with curriculum and intervention providers, 94

policy makers and, 94–95

taking stock, 92–93

self-awareness, as core SEL competency, 5, 6

self-control skills, 10–11, 12, 38

behavioral aspects of, 10–11

behaviors reflecting absence of, 35–36

components of, 35

Defining SEL worksheet category, 13*t*, 14

mental aspects of, kinds of, 10

mental dimensions of, measuring, 35

methods suited to measurement of, 35–36

see also grit

self-efficacy, 11

self-management, as core SEL competency, 5, 6

self-report, 28

description of, and assessment goal, 31*t*

description of, strengths and limitations, 30*t*

grit and, 36

mental dimensions of self-control and, 35

self-talk, self-control and, 10

SEL programs

evidence-based, 65

improved student outcomes and, 62

SEL skills

CASEL model, 5, 6

identifying candidate assessments, 38

important, identifying, 1–2

models other than CASEL's model, 5

that matter most, deciding on, 11–12, 14

SEL skills, organizing, 8–11

comprehension, 9, 12

execution, 9–10, 12

overview, 8

self-control, 10–11, 12

"serious games," 88

short-term memory, 35

social and emotional comprehension, methods suited to measurement of, 32–33

social and emotional learning (SEL), 56

defining, 2–3

definitional uncertainty surrounding, 58

finalizing your definition of, 14–15

identifying one model/theory as starting point, 5, 7–8

major components of, 5, 6

social and emotional learning (SEL)
(*continued*)
skills described in definition of, 8
strengths-based approach to, xxiv
team for developing clear operational
definition of, 3–4, 5, 11
social awareness, as core SEL competency,
5, 6
social behaviors
negative, 10
positive, 9–10
social-emotional comprehension, 9
social emotional skills, methods for assessing, 30t
social problems, solving, 9
Spencer Foundation, 94
standard scores, interpreting, 76
stigma, risk of, parental concern about, 63
structural validity, 45
summative assessment, xx, 17
systemic biases, 62

teacher professional development experiences, 88
teacher report
description of, and assessment goal, 31t
description of, strengths and limitations, 30t
teachers
commitment to action and, 89
social and emotional outcomes and, 56
team, for developing operational definition of SEL, 3–4, 5, 11. *see also* data
review team

team data review, producing, 79
testable hypotheses, generating, 84, 85
test companies, SEL assessments offered
by, 94
test data, team review of, 79
test-retest reliability, 41, 42, 43
test score equivalence, kinds of, 48–49
thinking skills, 9. *see also* comprehension
skills
training, interactive technologies for, 88
transparency, with parents, 59
treatment validity, 45, 46
trust, between parents and educators, 64
T scores, 76–77

validity, 39, 43–46
convergent, 44
criterion-related, 44–45, 46
definition of, 43
discriminant, 44
face, 44
reliability *vs.*, 43
structural, 45
treatment, 45, 46
validity evidence, taking measure of, 45–46
videos, instructional, 88

working groups, for maximizing SEL
assessment, 93
working memory, 35
worksheets
Assessment Selection, 54t
Data Use Needs Assessment, 70t
Defining SEL, 13t

About the Author

Clark McKown, Ph.D., is an associate professor of behavioral sciences at Rush University Medical Center (RUMC) and past executive director of the Rush NeuroBehavioral Center, a nationally recognized children's center supporting children's social and emotional development through clinical service, educational outreach, and research. He is also founder and president of xSEL Labs, whose mission is to improve student outcomes by helping educators understand children's social-emotional strengths and needs. Dr. McKown is a nationally recognized leader in the field of SEL assessment. He is a member of the steering committee of the Practical Social and Emotional Competence Assessment Work Group, a collaborative of leaders in research and practice working to advance the field of SEL assessment. McKown has been principal investigator on several federal and foundation grants whose purpose was to design, develop, validate, and scale social and emotional assessment systems. Findings from his research have been published in top-tier peer-reviewed scientific journals, including *Psychological Assessment, Journal of School Psychology,* and *Child Development*. McKown received his B.A. in psychology from Yale and his Ph.D. in psychology from UC Berkeley.